SPIRITU~

THE END OF THE AGE

By Jess Gjerstad

2

Cover photo by Jacob Allabach

Spiritual Warfare at the End of the Age

Copyright 2013 Jess Gjerstad

Printed by: CreateSpace an Amazon.com company
Charleston SC
 www.CreateSpace.com

In referring to "satan"- the name is normally left un-capitalized even
to the point of violating a grammatical rule.

<u>ACKNOWLEDGEMENTS</u>

I want to thank Mike Bickle and the IHOP-KC leadership team, the IHOP-KC staff, my parents, my sister, and those who have partnered financially and partnered in prayer with me through the years. Great is your reward in heaven.

Most of all, I want to thank the Author and Finisher of my faith.

5

Table of Contents

Forward
Introduction: We are in a fight!

FORWARD

 I would strongly recommend this book for anyone interested in spiritual warfare. This is not a book on casting out demons, nor is it a book on how to do deliverance. No, this is a book with some strong foundational teaching as well as some great spiritual insight on spiritual warfare. It's a must read if you desire to understand the times we are living in and what is needed to walk as an overcomer.

Tim Erickson
Associate Director of Deliverance @ IHOPKC

<u>INTRODUCTION</u>

The term "spiritual warfare" brings up many emotions and experiences. Some argue that spiritual warfare is simply a "cop out" to avoiding the real issue at hand. Other people are obsessed over the subject and believe that spiritual victories or defeats are behind every minor activity on the earth. Spiritual warfare brings out excitement and anticipation in some, while in it stirs up fear of the unknown in others. Many things have been done in the name of "spiritual warfare" from the humorous (people recklessly dancing with swords) to the heroic.

Our generation is more aware of supernatural activity than generations past. The Kingdom of God is advancing among the nations with an increase in prophetic encounters from God, healing, and deliverance in Jesus Christ. At the same time, there is a rising tide of brokenness, oppression, and wickedness inspired by satan and his demonic kingdom. The two kingdoms are on a collision course at the end of the age.

In the midst of the fight, we can learn things about the warrior king, Jesus Christ, we would learn in no other way. While not discounting strategic prophetic actions "in the moment" of worship gatherings and prayer meetings, spiritual warfare is a long-term activity we all engage in- whether we are aware of it or not. As we explore the topic of our spiritual warfare we need to look at the physical material aspects, the invisible spiritual dynamics, and a little bit on how they inter-react. We will look at some of the basic schemes of the enemy and how to fight and be victorious in Christ to the glory of God.

In part 1, we will look at some of the foundational questions related to the problem of evil: In the midst of the reality of pain and suffering, is there a God who fights for us? What is this spiritual warfare all about anyway? How we understand the supernatural realm and its relationship with the physical, material world we live in makes a difference on what we do to survive and even thrive in this spiritual war zone called earth.

In part 2, we look at the issue of identity since most of satan's evil schemes are about ruining our understanding of who God is and who we are to God in Christ Jesus. If satan boldly tempted Jesus related to His identity, why shouldn't we expect the same thing from our spiritual adversary? Understanding who God is and how valuable we are to God is key to walking in humility and triumphing over the enemy's schemes by the grace of God.

In part 3, we will look at the issue of spiritual authority and the enemy's counterfeit spiritual authority through witchcraft. God has all-surpassing power to back up the use of our authority in Christ under His leadership. However, satan and his demonic forces usurp authority through hidden areas of compromise. We want to explore why we are vulnerable and offer some understanding toward a scriptural remedy.

In part 4, we will look at how we can join together and fight the fight of faith on behalf of others. We often influence each other in unperceived ways and we can either bring harm or healing to others, based upon if we honor each other. There are also often unperceived battles related to the release of wealth and physical resources for the sake of the Kingdom. Together, we can fight for the removal of spiritual blindness over our family members and friends.

In part 5, we will look at some of the spiritual warfare lessons we can learn from the Book of Daniel. Daniel lived in the seductive culture of Babylon and stayed true to God. Daniel also faced off against the bitter envy of others, stirred up by the enemy. Daniel's prophetic visions give insight into demonic princes and schemes that blind many related to the supernatural realm. Daniel saw a final battle over who the nations will worship and we finish by looking at what scripture says about this final battle.

Our world is a war zone but we do not have to be victims. The Apostle Paul instructed Timothy to fight the good fight of faith. Understanding the hidden conflict brings greater personal fruitfulness and can change the destiny of our communities, and the nations. My hope and prayer is that you can learn how to be victorious through Christ Jesus in the midst of the battle.

PART I:

UNDERSTANDING THE WARZONE

1

WHEN LOVE MEANS WAR

No one likes pain and suffering. Christians often blame the devil for their own poor choices. Any discussion of spiritual warfare needs to include a broader discussion about sin, suffering, and the problem of evil. *"Why is there pain, sorrow, and suffering if God is good, and all-powerful/wise?"*

The problem of evil affects the mind, our emotions, our physical bodies and our overall well-being in a deep way.

Humanistic philosophies have tried to explain the problem of evil. Atheism and agnosticism argues that suffering and pain exist because we live in a "dog eats dog" world, a product of natural selection, probability, and statistics devoid of a sovereign hand. New Age philosophy takes it a step further and says we can become little "gods" through spiritual evolution.

Meanwhile, world religions tackle the problem in vain as well: Buddhism says that suffering and pain is caused by desire. If we can be without desire, then we can eliminate suffering and pain. Hinduism says that suffering is the result of bad "karma" and to try harder this time. Animistic societies believe that pain, suffering, and evil is completely the result of invisible spirits. Islam agrees that the problem of evil exists and that God also exists. However, Islam depicts God as a great task master and the kindness and goodness of God is absent. Does the Bible give us any hints?

Creation at rest: a time before there was spiritual conflict

"Remember the Sabbath and keep it Holy" is possibly the most neglected commandment in the Western Church. God formed the human frame with the desire for rest, but there is something deeper happening. Understanding the Sabbath is far deeper than simply worshipping Jesus together on Saturday versus a Sunday. The religious leaders made legalistic requirements and then accused Jesus of violating the Sabbath because his disciples were picking grain in a field and eating it on the Sabbath. In doing so, they completely missed the original intention of the Sabbath. This commandment is pointing to something far more important than simply taking a day off.

The Sabbath began before there was the problem of sin or warfare in humanity. To illustrate, I was at my nephew Andrew's wedding to Becky in 2012. The setting was perfectly prepared to the family's liking. The wedding ceremony was set on a baseball diamond and the pastor was dressed as the umpire. We were all set to "play ball" – and we had a blast of a wedding party.

Of course, if anyone has been part of planning a wedding-you know that it is an incredibly important and sometimes arduous task. There are the issues of announcements, wedding party participants, invitations, the ceremony, the wedding reception (including food, gifts, drinks, and other activities), pictures/media and the honeymoon. The catered food needs to be in place on time, the gifts organized, and the dance floor ready along with the disc jockey. Meanwhile, there is the clashing of different family values and personalities. Often so much needs to be done administratively with deadlines that the family will hire a wedding coordinator.

Before time, God the Father, Son, and Holy Spirit have been preferring each other, honoring each other, serving each other, and glorifying each other throughout all of eternity. As expressions of fiery, extravagant love, The Father, Son, and Holy Spirit have desired to give each other something in humanity. God wanted a bride, a royal family, and individual creatures like us to participate in the eternal joy of the fellowship with our Trinitarian God.

I desire to love.

Genesis 1 describes the creation of the heavens and the earth: Jesus spoke out what was in the heart of God the Father and at the sound of His voice, God the Holy Spirit acted in power. Creation came forth in all its splendor. Job 38 describes the angels staring at this spectacle of creation with singing and shouts of joy. There was no spiritual warfare- all creation was at peace.

However, all of this was leading up to the crowning moment of physical creation- that sixth day when God created man in His image. Like a grand party, God prepared all of physical creation for man-but there was still anticipation-like a groom anticipating seeing his bride in her bridal gowns. What would the first people do in seeing God's face and his creation?

We need to ask, "Why did God bless that seventh day and make it Holy?" Initially, Scripture is vague about what happened on that 7th day. It simply says,

By the seventh day, God had finished the work he had been doing; so that on the seventh day he rested from all his work. And God blessed the seventh day and made it holy, because on it he rested from all the work of creating that he had done. (Genesis 2:2-3).

God made it sacred because something so special happened on that day between God and man that God treasures it forever. God says in Luke 15 that when one person repents, there is immediately a great rejoicing in heaven. We can only imagine that first day when man and God openly rejoiced and loved each other without the presence of sin, shame, or darkness.

As Adam and Eve spent more time in the garden ruling over the created order on earth, each day they were presented with a choice: Would they wait upon God to walk with them in the cool of the evening to get the answers they wanted or would they attempt to get all the answers themselves, independent of God's wisdom through eating from the tree of knowledge of good and evil. Would they choose God's wisdom and ways or would they choose their own wisdom?

How can a good God send people to an eternal hell?

Pop culture falsely depicts the God of the Bible as a giant "kill-joy" threatening those who rebel against His rules with death (often by lightning bolts) and then eternal hell. Sadly, pre-Christians perceive the doctrine of sin and eternal judgment as a method to control peoples' behavior to what those in authority want- to maintain order (and get benefits such as money, and other resources). No wonder why people want nothing to do with this "god"!

Ignored in the whole conversation is- what are we as human being doing when we choose selfishness at the expense of God and other people? The Psalmist writes:

You open your hand and satisfy the desires of every living thing. The LORD is righteous in all his ways and loving toward all he has made. (Psalm 145:16-17)

To say it another way, God gives to everyone what they want-even if they don't realize what they are asking for. The problem is that our human hearts are deceitful and selfish- usually at the expense of our long-term good individually and as a people. Romans 1:20-32 and Genesis 3-6 describes the sad spiral of sin leading to depravity and eternal torment.

In Genesis 3, Adam and Eve disobeyed God by eating from the Tree of the Knowledge of Good and Evil. Originating from celestial evil, humanity was tricked into joining the rebellion against God. They engaged in false pleasures apart from the superior pleasures found in knowing God. Things went downhill when Adam blamed Eve (who in turned blamed the snake). The original sin had grown into sinful selfishness at the expense of others cloaked in deceit and blame shifting.

Things got worse with Cain and Abel. Cain was tending the fields (the "cool job" reminding him of the original call) while Abel was tending flocks (animals were only used as sacrifices and were not eaten until Genesis 9), a constant reminder of the penalty for sin. In a great reversal, God clearly approved of Abel's animal offering while disapproving of Cain's offering in Genesis 4. Instead of humbling himself before God and Abel, Cain became very angry and bitter at what had just happened. Sin had increased from simple selfishness to bitterness and hatred. It was out of bitterness that Cain openly rejected God's counsel and warning.

In rejecting God's counsel, Cain cut himself off from God's grace. Sin then exploded outwardly as he decided to strike Abel down. As Cain was killing Abel, he surely heard his brother's agonizing screams and writhing in pain. After God confronted Cain, he lied to God's face and then asked a famous (defiant) question:

"I don't know," he replied. "Am I my brother's keeper?"
(Genesis 4:9)

God pronounced judgment upon him, saying that he was now under a curse- he would be forced live by taking from others.

In the next generation, Lamech also killed someone- who had wounded him…and then justified his actions before other people. In this way, Lamech went further by teaching others that it was okay to murder and get revenge. From Lamech's story we learn that people who have been hurt by sin and poisoned by bitterness end up hurting others (often far worse than they were hurt) in their search for "justice". By Genesis 6, the earth was filled with bitter cries of wickedness, violence, and hatred.

Could you imagine what earth would be like if God had not limited humanity's lifespan and people lived forever in this horrible state? The Lake of Fire is the simply a geographical location where all can see the final expression of the fullness of sin and the full effects of sin. To provide hope and guard humanity's future, God banished Adam and Eve from the Garden of Eden and put high-ranking angels with flaming swords to guard the way back to the Tree of Life.

Meanwhile the scripture tells us that God desires no one to go to hell (Ezekiel 18:32). Hell was created for the devil and his angels who instigated the rebellion with all its suffering, pain, and sorrow. People choose to go there through their persistent sinful choices-including rejecting God's solution in Christ Jesus (not realizing the consequences). With great sorrow, God gives them what they "wanted".

When love means war: the God who fights for us.

Even in the midst of the pain and sorrow of Genesis 3, God remembered that first day with humanity. After the disaster in the garden, Love would simply not give up. God would go to war on behalf of humanity. Paul briefly describes his conquest:

Christ Jesus:
   Who being in very nature God,
      did not consider equality with God something to be grasped,
   but made himself nothing,
      taking the very nature of a servant,
      being made in human likeness.
   And being found in appearance as a man,
      he humbled himself
      and became obedient to death-even death on a cross! (Philippians 2:5-8)

Most warriors throughout history have conquered to oppress or for bragging rights. Satan and evil is simply no match for God, He could just speak and wipe evil out. However, Jesus fought to redeem us and win our hearts back for the glory of His Father.

John depicts Jesus as the Lamb of God slain from the foundation of the world. Behind God's atonement over our sin, and desire to win humanity back out of love for us, the cross is a statement of what has always been between God the Son and God the Father that they share together with the Holy Spirit in perfect unity: *"I would rather suffer to the depths for you than see your dreams go unfulfilled."* The cross is God the Father, Son, and Holy Spirit's statement of longsuffering love. It is also a statement of God's hatred of sin and love for humanity. See Hebrews 12:1-3; Luke 15 and John 12:23-29. There is so much that could be said about the depths of suffering that God the Father, Son, and Holy Spirit endured to win lost and condemned humanity back to Himself.

Scripture tells us that God has prepared a resting place for those who will enter into the Kingdom of God. Jesus even said that in His Father's house, there are many rooms. Hebrews 4 instructs us to do whatever it takes to enter into God's rest. Revelation 21 and 22 describes that this ultimate glory of redemption when Heaven to come to earth. The Kingdom of God is coming-heaven is preparing to invade earth to permanently restore it.

Human civilization arrogantly continues to ask the question: *"Why is there pain, sorrow, and suffering if God is good, and all-powerful/wise?"* The question needs to be answered by a different question from a humble heart: *Why does an all-powerful God willingly suffer long with our selfish rebellion and wickedness to show kindness towards us?*

Jesus Christ, the ultimate warrior has fought and broke through so that we could be reconciled to God. God has offered us a new identity from sinners to Sons of God, part of the royal family forever. God has offered us a new nature- one that can enjoy the superior pleasures of unending love and righteousness in Christ Jesus. God has offered us a new destiny- from eternal destruction, agony, and horror to eternal pleasure, honor, and wholeness. What then shall we do?

Peter replied, "Repent and be baptized, every one of you, in the name of Jesus for the forgiveness of your sins. And you will receive the gift of the Holy Spirit. The promise is for you and your children and for all who are far off- for all whom the Lord our God will call.
(Acts 2:38-39)

If you have never turned your life over to Jesus, now is the time to do it. Even as God gave his all in love to fight for us, God is now asking us all to surrender everything back to Him and join His family forever.

Our current fight of faith: that the Lamb would receive His eternal reward!

For those who have turned to Jesus and experienced His love, our battle is now slightly different. If we have truly received this great love, what else makes any sense than to return it? In response to the challenge related to what the greatest commandment is, we read:

Jesus replied, "'Love the Lord your God with all your heart and with all your soul and with all your mind. This is the first and greatest commandment. And the second is like it: 'Love your neighbor has yourself.' All the Law and the Prophets hang on these two commandments." (Matthew 22:37-39)

Jesus Christ gave us the greatest commandment, the greatest challenge, the most rewarding commandment, and the greatest promise. The Moravians gave up everything to love Jesus and spread His love to those who are in need. Their battle cry: *"Give to the Lamb the reward of His suffering!"* Practically what does this look like?

The Sermon on the Mount (Matthew 5-7) gives us insight into what it is like to love God with everything we have. The "Be Attitudes" of Matthew 5:3-10 describe what a heart completely set ablaze with loving Jesus looks like. The Sermon on the Mount then highlights six threats (bitterness/hatred, immoral lust, unfaithfulness, deception, greed, and fear) to our hearts along with five activities (prayer with the word, fasting for the sake of others, extravagant giving, serving without price, forgiving and blessing enemies) that will cause us together to walk in passion and victory in Jesus Christ.

Hence the battle- deep within the heart of every true follower of Jesus is a desire to walk this out on earth. However, anyone who has attempted to do this consistently knows it is a tremendous fight. Scripture highlights three obstacles we fight.

The first foe that we fight is our own sinful flesh and the law of sin operating in our own lives. Even though our spirit has been made new by the power of the Holy Spirit, our souls and physical bodies are still broken. Sin still wants to grow and cause destruction. The Holy Spirit wants to "break out" to bring wholeness to our souls and physical bodies. However, this is often a slow and painful process. We must take up our cross and follow Jesus daily.

The second foe that we face is "the world"-a hostile environment consisting of broken (and sometimes hostile) people along with a creation that is broken. When we were little, swimming to get to the other side of the pool was hard enough. Battling the world and the flesh is often like swimming to the other side of a swimming pool- but the pool is a wave pool and the waves and current is against us.

Most of global culture is self-centered and selfish- under the power of "the god of this age". People who choose to walk in obedience to Jesus are often viewed as weak and prime targets to get stomped on by the world. In attempting to walk out deep obedience to Jesus, inevitably, we will be going against much of the flow of the culture.

The third obstacle that we face is the devil and his demonic hordes. We face an organized foe that has malevolent intentions. He will attempt to take advantage of the weakness of sinful flesh along with energizing already painful, difficult circumstances caused by our environment to do us in. Jesus has given us authority over this foe. However, simply rebuking the devil only removes the demonic "energizing" effect- we still need to deal with the world and the flesh using the wisdom from heaven.

Thankfully, we are not alone. Jesus Christ is seated at the right hand of the Father. On the other hand, we are the Body of Christ. Our spiritual warfare is simply an extension of His spiritual warfare to bring redemption to individuals, communities, and the entire earth.

2
THE WAR OF WISDOM

"Spiritual warfare is about wisdom, not about power."

In the summer of 2004, I had been on the full-time staff of IHOP-KC for less than a year. In 2004 IHOP-KC was relatively small with roughly 400 people that functioned as a family-we all knew each other fairly well. We had just lost a dear member of our community in a battle with cancer. In the midst of our corporate grieving, Julie Meyer had a beautiful prophetic encounter that brought great comfort to our family.

A few weeks later, Julie Meyer again had a prophetic experience in July related to Daniel 12:4. Here is some of the staff email the leadership shared with the entire community related to Julie's prophetic visitation:

DEAR IHOP FAMILY
Julie Meyer had a visitation of the Lord in which she saw an angel visit IHOP and Mike Bickle - the angel gave Julie "Dan. 12:4" to give to Mike in response to fasting for 30 days. This is most remarkable in that Julie did not know that Mike had been praying (for 3 months) on a near daily basis for Dan. 12:4 to be released…

As a spiritual family we are dedicating 30 days (July 25-Aug. 24) to seek the Lord with fasting. This fast will vary for everyone, but for many it will involve fasting related to food, entertainment, media, unnecessary socializing and ministry leadership meetings. We all want to be in IHOP as much as possible for these 30 days. The fast will finish just before the all staff meeting at 4:00 P.M. on Tuesday, Aug. 24. The staff meeting will be a time of sharing what has been happening in the 30 days.

Daniel had been seeking more prophetic understanding from the angel in Daniel 12. However, the angel basically indicated that the full understanding would be for another generation:

Those who are wise will shine like the brightness of the heavens, and those who lead many to righteousness, like the stars forever and ever. But you, Daniel, close up and seal the words of the scroll until the time of the end. Many will go here and there to increase knowledge. (Daniel 12:4)

We believed that God wanted to give skill to the Body of Christ to understand the end-times. Prophetic understanding leads to greater confidence in the midst of the events surrounding the return of Jesus to the earth. In faith, we went on a corporate 30 day fast for greater understanding of these end-time passages of scripture for our generation.

An encounter with "Wisdom"

Near the end of the corporate fast, I went to the prayer room on a Friday morning. I was ready for the fast to be over and meditating on James 3:

Who is wise among and understanding among you? Let him show it by his good life, by deeds done in the humility that comes from wisdom. But if you harbor bitter envy and selfish ambition in your hearts, do not boast about it or deny the truth. Such "wisdom" does not come down from heaven but is earthly, unspiritual, of the devil. For where you have envy and selfish ambition, there you find disorder and every evil practice. But wisdom that comes from heaven is first of all pure; then peace loving, considerate, submissive, full of mercy and good fruit, impartial and sincere. Peace makers who sow in peace raise a harvest of righteousness.
(James 3:13-18)

The word WISE was highlighted by the Holy Spirit. Suddenly scripture after scripture flashed in front of my face: Ephesians 3:10-12; Matthew 7:21-24; Daniel 7:7; Revelation 13:18; Daniel 12:3-4 and many others.

I was stunned and terrified at this- here I was, perhaps the most arrogant and immature of anyone in the whole community and God had just given me a key to understanding the spiritual warfare at the end of the age. At this I was left in turmoil. I knew that there was way too much of "the wisdom of satan" (selfishness at the expense of other people) in me. I also knew that I could do nothing to get rid of it. Flesh will only give birth to flesh; it would take the Holy Spirit in power to change things around (see John 3:1-8).

The next day, I had originally planned to go to hear Mark Anderson talk on city-wide transformation. However, I felt the Holy Spirit let me know that I was not to be there that night. Instead, I was to go over to Doria's home contemplative group.

At the end of the contemplative time, Cheryl Doria began explaining about Heidi Baker and the children she trained to pray for the sick-in how they were releasing miracles. She then asked if anyone needed prayer for physical healing. I said I needed it. Suddenly, the presence of the Holy Spirit came upon me in a very powerful way.

I was then caught up in a trance. I could hear what was going on around me, (people were still praying) but I couldn't respond to them- It was like I was in another place. A beautiful man-Christ Jesus approached me. He was shining brighter than the sun and wearing a beautiful shining robe. I could tell He had tears in His eyes.

Jesus then said, *"Do you realize what you've been asking for?"* (He was obviously referring to the release of the manifold wisdom of God in my life-the glory of humility.) His voice was quivering with tears of joy.

I said, (tears running down my cheeks) "No"

Jesus then said, *"You have asked for a gift that I have longed to give My people for centuries. I will help you to receive this."* Instantly James 1:5 flashed across my mind.

If any of you lacks wisdom, he should ask God, who gives generously to all without finding fault, and it will be given to him. But when he asks, he must believe and not doubt, because he who doubts is like a wave of the sea, blown and tossed by the wind. That man should not think he will receive anything from the Lord; he is a double minded man, unstable in all he does (James 1:5).

The trance ended and I laid there numb and "out of it" for well over half an hour.

At first, this fast seemed insignificant as not much happened from this fast. However, out of this community-wide 30 day fast, God released two very important keys to understand spiritual warfare. In this chapter we will look at a key of wisdom. In the next chapter, we will look at a key revelation.

So what is this war really all about?

From Daniel 10, we get our first clear glimpses of cosmic spiritual warfare: angels and demons fighting it out related to the rise and fall of world empires. This leads to a whole bunch of questions such as: *What is this war all about?* And, *how did this war get started anyway?* And, *"Is there a way for us to practically be victorious in spiritual warfare?"*

Satan accused God that his wisdom and ways (selfishness at the expense of others) was superior to God's wisdom (centered around humility and servant-hood). Scripture indicates that up to 1/3rd of all the angelic hosts of heaven believed satan and thus rebelled against God.

Satan cannot compete with God in terms of power. The difference in available power and authority between Creator God and any creature (whether it be an archangel or an ant) is endless. God could easily destroy satan and his hordes- but that would not answer the question before the high courts of heaven and the earth if God's wisdom was indeed superior to satan's wisdom. Is there a way to prove God's wisdom is supreme in producing pleasure?

God made human beings in His image with a dream in His heart for us. His original intent was that we would make known the manifold wisdom of God to all of creation: We are the ones who have the honor from God to prove that His wisdom is supreme over satan's wisdom *regardless of the circumstances.* However, when Adam sinned and joined the rebellion against God, he gave the authority he enjoyed over earth away to satan. The world is in chaos because of that terrible decision.

It was the 2nd Adam, Jesus Christ who regained the authority over the earth from satan at the cross. However, before Jesus went to the cross, He said that He would not use that power and authority to establish His physical kingdom on earth until 1.) The Gospel had gone to every ethnic group (Matthew 24:10) and 2.) The Jewish leadership in Jerusalem personally invite Him back to be their King (Matthew 23:37-39). Satan knows this and has used his trickery, deception, and usurped human power/authority to resist these two items to the utter-most extreme.

At the core, spiritual warfare is about wisdom- the wisdom of Heaven (from God) versus the wisdom of this world (from satan). James 3 highlights this clash of wisdom:

Who is wise among and understanding among you? Let him show it by his good life, by deeds done in the humility that comes from wisdom. *But if you harbor bitter envy and selfish ambition in your hearts, do not boast about it or deny the truth. Such "wisdom" does not come down from heaven but is earthly, unspiritual, of the devil. For where you have envy and selfish ambition, there you find disorder and every evil practice. But* **_wisdom that comes from heaven is first of all pure; then peace loving, considerate, submissive, full of mercy_**

and good fruit, impartial and sincere. Peace makers who sow in peace raise a harvest of righteousness. (James 3:13-18)

The two types of wisdom are sharply contrasted: The wisdom of heaven centers around humility, honoring God, and other people- even at the costly or painful expense of selfishness. The other type of wisdom focuses around selfishness at the expense of others.

Spiritual warfare is about the clash of wisdom, not power: *Which type of wisdom is supreme in producing pleasure to the human spirit, soul, mind, and body?* Jesus contrasted wisdom verses foolish: the wise builder vs. the foolish builder (Matthew 7:21-24), the wise virgins vs. the foolish virgins (Matthew 25:1-10).

So here we are as human beings, caught in the midst of this spiritual war zone called earth. The problem is that we automatically are disposed to choose the wisdom of this world over the wisdom of God because of the curse passed down from Adam (i.e. called the law of sin). However, once we are born again, that curse is broken and we are free to choose the wisdom of God (centered around humility and serving others) or going back and choosing the wisdom of satan (selfishness at other's expense). Satan no longer has rights to force us to do anything through the name of Jesus (though he may seem awfully strong). Meanwhile, God rarely "forces" anyone to do something either. The choice is ours.

Understanding the leadership of Jesus:

So here we are in the present- It's clear that Jesus is much more powerful than satan- and that Jesus will triumph over evil in an ultimate sense. However, in the practical, day-to day living, it is often much easier to live selfishly than under the leadership of Jesus-which at times does not make sense. Many people stumble over the leadership of Jesus. Here is an edited version of a "political endorsement" written in the midst of the 2008 Presidential election:

Having spent significant time with this man on the earth, I can tell you that "Cephas Stumble" is genuinely the kindest, most humble leader I have ever met. He never compromises His ethical standards. He responds affirmatively to those who are truly loyal but He is not manipulated to do things by offers of big money, fulfillment of "pork-barrel projects", or special honor. He is supremely confident in His leadership decisions. However, He genuinely enjoys showing kindness to those who are in pain, and have broken lives. His willingness to radically sacrifice to solve what He calls the "fundamental problem" of the human race is astounding.

What makes things really confusing is that His leadership methods often cause more pain in the short-term than relief. First, most of the people on His leadership team always appear to be so weak, frail, and "unqualified". Some of the people who are on His leadership team include the equivalent of an IRS agent, a few fishermen, a soldier, and a poor widow. He does have some doctors, writers, and lawyers on His leadership team, but they are surprisingly few.

His leadership style often doesn't make much sense- As a man of "no reputation", He is not afraid to allow His leadership team to get humiliated. He often allows rebels who blatantly oppose His leadership and ethical standards to go unpunished. Meanwhile, He often disciplines those on His leadership team, holding them accountable to His leadership ethics, including His demand to lead in meekness and serving with others in mind.

He doesn't seem too concerned about public opinion or about what the so-called "political experts" say about His leadership. In fact, He often offends His closet friends with His cutting words. His speeches are brilliant but confusing. He uses such simple vocabulary, but He seems to say such profound things. He often talks about this "fundamental problem" that developed when a former mystical friend rose up and arrogantly said that He was smarter than anyone in the universe and became "the adversary".

As military commander-in chief, "Cephas Stumble" appears to be brilliant but baffling. His intelligence of the adversaries is incredible. It appears that He always knows what His enemies are thinking and doing. He seems to either know or even create weather patterns and natural phenomena in advance. We still don't know how Israel got out of Egypt. Their footsteps seemingly end at one side of the Red Sea, and then continue on the other side. He claims responsibility for pulling off stunts with the sun that threw off NASA's space flight calculations for years. I've heard many reports of how He gave specific information about earthquakes, weather patterns, cosmic disturbances, and many other "strange" events.

As the leader of the military, He ordered one guy to lead an army in marching around a city seven times before it collapsed to the ground. He ordered another guy to take 300 men with trumpets and glass jars to go and give the enemy a "wake up call" in the middle of the night to defeat him. He told another guy to put the equivalent of the "Marine Corp Band" and the "Brooklyn Tabernacle Choir" out front as part of a military strategy for victory.

What is really confusing about His military leadership is that sometimes, He allows His adversaries to win, resulting in great humiliation for those of us who claim to endorse His leadership. Most of the time, He claims it is part of his overall leadership plan involving the discipline of His leadership team for ignoring His *leadership ethics and strategies. However, there are cases where the consequences of losing are so devastating to so many people that this explanation simply does not make any sense-until 10, 20, 50, 100's or even 1000's of years later.*

He doesn't seem too concerned about losing battles (that seem so big). "Cephas Stumble" always seems supremely confident that He will ultimately lead the way and win politically, militarily, and culturally. The only people He wants on His leadership team must share His unwavering confidence even in the darkest and most troubling circumstances. In order to qualify them for leadership, it seems that "Cephas Stumble" deliberately puts them in difficult, painful, and disillusioning situations as opportunities to prove their loyalty to Him.

The culmination of this clash of wisdom at the end of the age:
Jesus gave the parable of the weeds in Matthew 13:24-30. God's people continue to sow righteousness based upon the wisdom of God and the people of this earth (energized by demonic power) continue to sow wickedness based on the wisdom of satan. At the end of the age, Jesus warned everything would be harvested-both the fruit of God's wisdom (righteousness) and the fruit of satan's wisdom (wickedness).

Scripture tells us a great deal related to the culmination of satan's wisdom. First, both the book of Daniel and Revelation depict a global empire that displays the fullness of depraved human nature:

"After that, in my vision at night I looked, and there before me was a forth beast-terrifying and frightening and very powerful. It had large iron teeth; it crushed and devoured its victims and trampled underfoot whatever was left. It was different from all the former beasts and it had 10 horns." (Daniel 7:7)

In observing the created order, Charles Darwin observed things such as "natural selection", competition, and violence. Simply put, the strong survive by oppressing and crushing the weak. Without the wisdom of God, humanity simply operates like the animal kingdom- the strong oppress the weak which will result in the greatest human atrocities in history. Daniel even saw the saints being handed over to be persecution and martyrdom at the hands of this most wicked empire at the very end.

Second, Revelation 17-18 describes "Mystery Babylon" as a harlot who seduces the nations of the earth. As the human race, we have learned that working together, we can accomplish a whole lot more than what we can accomplish individually- this is what the tower of Babel was all about. The Harlot Babylon is all about using people for our own ends- and then discarding people as if they are only worth what they could produce for us. These two systems will affect the spiritual, political, economic, military, and relational fabric of society on the earth to bring the heights of misery and pain on the earth at the end of the age.

Isaiah prophesied that God will use the darkness to highlight His bright, radiant wisdom through His people. The unfaithfulness of the Harlot Babylon is in sharp contrast to the faithful, radiant Church operating as the Bride that Jesus will raise up at the end of the age for the great wedding celebration of the Lamb. Ephesians 5 tells us that Jesus will wash the Bride with the water of His word to prepare her in bright, righteousness.

In the midst of the backdrop of the most pain and sorrow caused by the wisdom of satan will be a joy-filled victorious Church. Psalm 45 tells us that Jesus was anointed with the oil of joy because he loves righteousness and hates wickedness. In the midst of the greatest tribulation, God will enable a lovesick, joy-filled people to experience the heights of righteousness, joy, and peace in the Holy Spirit. They will make known the superiority of the manifold wisdom of God for all of creation to see.

Choose wisely!

So the choices are now ours: the wisdom of God or the wisdom of satan. However scripture gives us a warning and a promise:

Therefore, brothers, we have an obligation-but it is not to the sinful nature, to live according to it. For if you live according to the sinful nature, you will die; but if by the Spirit you put to death the misdeeds of the body, you will live, because those who are led by the Spirit of God are sons of God. (Romans 8:12-14)

What we consistently choose and how deeply we make our choices determines our eternal destiny at the judgment seat of Christ. Our final appointment with Jesus is by far the most important one- we must get ready.

3

ON EARTH AS IT IS IN HEAVEN

It is quite possibly the most frequently prayer heard in Church. The Lutheran Church I was raised in prayed it every single Sunday:

Our Father in Heaven, Hallowed be your name. Your Kingdom come, your will be done on earth as it is in heaven. Give us today our daily bread. Forgive us our debts, as we also have forgiven our debtors. And lead us not into temptation, but deliver us from the evil one. (Matthew 6:9-13)

Hidden within this prayer is one of the most profound secrets to understanding spiritual warfare.

In the last chapter, I told the story about when IHOP-KC went on a 30-day fast related to Daniel 12:3-4. Approximately nine months later, Mike Bickle began publicly teaching about the millennial kingdom and the throne of Jesus. In describing the supremacy of Jesus, Paul writes:

For God was pleased to have all his fullness dwell in him, and through him to reconcile to himself all things, whether things on earth or things in heaven, by making peace through his blood, shed on the cross. (Colossians 1:19-20)

And he made known to us the mystery of his will according to his good pleasure, which he purposed in Christ, to be put into effect when the times will have reached their fulfillment-to bring all things in heaven and on earth together under one head, even Christ.
(Ephesians 1:9-10)

Jesus will rule the heavens and the earth in the Millennial reign- without the influence of satan. However, Jesus rules the heavens and the earth today! Hidden in "plain view" is a critical key to understanding spiritual warfare at the end of the age: Our worldview must match the worldview of the Bible to effectively engage in spiritual battle.

The Hebraic mindset: the spiritual realm and the physical realm are inter-related

The Biblical viewpoint sees the physical, material, natural realm and the spiritual, supernatural realm together as one reality. Though not obvious at first, understanding this has several very important implications for how we follow Jesus.

1. *Actions in the physical material realm (including the righteous or sinful choices of people), affect the spiritual supernatural realm (Leviticus 18:24-28; 2 Chronicles 7:13-14; Romans 8:18-24 etc).*
We see evidence of this through *the transformations* videos with George Otis Jr. Generally the story line is that a nation is in peril because of its sin and idolatry. The people individually and corporately as a nation (governmental officials representing the nation) repent and fully turn their allegiance to Jesus Christ and then follow His wisdom and ways. God then "miraculously" heals the land with agricultural and environmental evidence. Crime and other social problems also suddenly vanish.

2. *Satan and the demonic realm have set up an alternative spiritual government in the heavenly realms that oppose the Kingdom of God* in the heavens and on the earth based upon his selfish wisdom (Ephesians 6:10-14; Daniel 10:18-20; Matthew 12:25-29 etc.).

3. *Since people are spirit, soul, and body- we can commune with God by the power of the Holy Spirit in worship and prayer and interact with the physical, material realm of earth.* Communing with God in worship and intercession (in the unseen spiritual realm) will affect what happens in the physical, material realm. In addition, demonic activity in the spiritual realm can also affect what happens in natural realm *if they can find agreement with people on the earth* through idolatry, sorcery, and practicing unrighteousness.

Greek mindset: the spiritual and the physical realms are separate

Meanwhile, much of Western Culture is built upon Greek culture and philosophy. Greek philosophy falsely divides the two realms and separates them- There is the physical, material realm and the unseen spirit realm. God is in heaven and people are on earth. Human beings can only directly interact with the physical, natural realm; and not affect the supernatural realm under the anointing of the Holy Spirit. An accusation that I frequently hear, *"You're so heavenly minded because you are no earthly good"* often reflects a Greek worldview mindset.

At first, the difference between a Hebraic worldview verses a Greek mindset does not appear to be very important- but it has subtle, deep implications:

1. *Greek philosophers taught that the physical material realm is bad but the pure "forms" are in "the heavens"- inaccessible to people.* Under this worldview philosophy, our spirits are inaccessible to evil. So it doesn't matter in the physical and material realm since what we do on the earth since heaven and earth are separated. It leads to a "false grace" message that we now have freedom to sin.

2. *A Greek mindset worldview diminishes the significance of partnering with Jesus in the labor of intercession.* If God does things automatically according to His will and we can't affect the decisions of God through intercession, why should we ask God to change things-and then believe that He consistently answers prayer? Indeed, secular humanism takes it a step further and says we don't even need God (because He doesn't exist).

3. *At the core, a Greek mindset worldview is built upon unbelief.* Within the result in modern culture is suspicious of any supernatural activity as being "of the devil" simply because they do not understand it and cannot control it.

Meanwhile, a post-modern un-churched generation understands that there is likely something behind the material, physical realm and is exploring it outside biblically safe boundaries through New Age and occult practices. (The Church is rejected as being "out of touch spiritually" and religious.) This leads to greater amounts of bondage and brokenness.

Without the understanding that we are all directly accountable to a benevolent Supernatural Creator we are left with humanism as the highest form of "good". Humanistic philosophy has led to a motto of "if it feels good, do it".

As the result, Western Culture has seen an explosion of sexual immorality in the last 50 years. With it has come an explosion in broken homes, murder (through abortion), and mistrust of authority. It is now really clear that satan has gained significant in-roads into destroying a culture that was once built upon Judeo-

Christian values. Worst of all, it has put millions of Christians in danger (who think they are saved) because scripture warns that those who practice unrepentant sin (including sexual immorality) will not inherit the Kingdom of God.

God's sovereign leadership in this age- the 4 winds of heaven in the midst of the sea of humanity

Obviously, God is the sovereign ruler over all the nations and people groups of the earth. Yet, have we stopped to consider how God intervenes in the affairs of men? Usually, if we find God *directly* stepping into intervene with someone, (i.e. not sending an angel, or a dream etc.) that person ends up dead. In His goodness towards people, we need to understand- So how does God lead the affairs of men- *while remaining hidden*? Even as God walked on the earth, He remained hidden to the natural eye, taking on human flesh.

Daniel 7 describes "the four winds" in how God is leading human history. This phrase is used nine different times in the Bible (Jeremiah 49:36; Ezekiel 37:9; Daniel 7:2, 8:8, 11:4; Zechariah 2:6; Matthew 24:31; Mark 13:27; Revelation 7:1)- usually related to gathering (His elect believers, Israel) or scattering (related to the nations). Two other passages relate to how empires grow towards the four winds of heaven (seemingly immune to God's hidden interventions). So what is this all about anyway?

In the midst of the sea of humanity, God is influencing history on a global scale in four ways while being intimately involved into our own personal lives:

1. *God is influences history through giving "divine technological ideas".* God prompts us by His Word and the Holy Spirit to do things with divine ideas. God will even prompt unbelievers and give them "divine ideas" to bring inventions and other developments into the sea of humanity to influence history on a global scale. For example, Bill Gates (not known if he is a believer) got an idea about "windows" that would make computing much faster and easier. The global result of this has been a digital revolution that deeply affects our lives. Where did that idea come from?

2. *Jesus is King over the natural realm- all of the rest of creation obeys Him.* Insurance agencies talk about "acts of God" (usually as an excuse why they don't need to pay up) related to the created order. God has set up the created order to be a blessing. All of the visible, natural created order obeys Jesus- except human beings whom God has given authority on the earth to.

However, due to man's sin, the earth and all creation continues to groan (Romans 8:22-25). The supernatural result of humanity's sin is that the earth thrown "out of balance". In trying to regain equilibrium, the result is earthquakes, hurricanes, droughts, tornadoes, etc. In the midst of the disasters, God is intricately involved in using the negative for the good of us individually, and for the Church as a whole. Of course, the correction of one imbalance creates more imbalances-so creation is never at "rest".

3. God is influencing us through the raising up of cultural and political leadership;

Scripture says that God either directly raises up people or allows them to be raised up as leaders (Exodus 9:13-17; 2 Samuel 5:12; Daniel 2:20-22; Psalm 75:5-7; Romans 13:1-2 etc.). The type of leadership (good, wise, unwise, evil) raised up is an indirect source of God's blessing or God's judgment upon the people. Just as God changed the heart of Nebuchadnezzar, God can change the hearts of kings-depending on how we respond to Him. This is one of the reasons why we are commanded to pray God's will for those in leadership.

4. War in the heavenlies: angels and demons battle it out.

Daniel 10, Revelation 12, and other passages of scripture give us glimpses of a heavenly battle: Satan and his demons verses Michael the arch-angel and his angelic warriors. This invisible spiritual battle influences the first three realms- the natural order, leaders, and technological or cultural developments. Sometimes, the supernatural realm breaks into the natural realm and we see healings, miracles, and other supernatural phenomena. Satan counters with his deceptive sorcery. Both the Kingdom of God (through the angelic realm) and the satan's kingdom (through the demonic realm) can influence the other three human realms that we can see. However, there must be agreement on the earth through people to do so at this time. Ultimately, satan will not overcome God and is unwittingly used by God to do His will.

Bear in mind that this is the same God who walked on the earth and died on the cross for our sins. Satan and his demons are still under the complete control of the Lord God Almighty. Satan and his demons may be influencing our world and making life difficult-all the while God is using him (unwittingly) to strengthen our faith and love.

He is the same God yesterday, today, and forever. God was still ruling both heaven and earth and He will be doing so forever. Satan's kingdom is only temporary as he will be bound in the bottomless pit and then thrown into the lake of fire. In the midst of the chaos, Jesus is still intimately working all things together for our good.

The role of prayer and worship- Greek worldview vs. Hebraic Worldview

Perhaps the greatest consequence of a Greek worldview verses a Hebraic worldview is directly related to how we interact with God in worship and intercession. Within the Western culture, it is very difficult to get the Body of Christ to go deep in communion with God simply because of a faulty belief system about the place of prayer. In a Greek worldview:

- God is in heaven and we are on the earth. God has given people delegated authority on earth (Psalm 115:16; Genesis 1:26-27), but not in heaven.

- God can intervene on earth whenever He desires. However, the heavens (supernatural realm of angels and demons) and the earth (physical, material realm) do not interact with each other in any predictable, regular fashion.

- God can intervene on earth whenever He desires. However, the intensity of the prayers of the saints or the degree of agreement on earth do not affect how God answers (or does not answer) prayer on the earth.

As the result, it has a tremendous impact on how the Church that is steeped in Western Culture understands the role of worship and prayer on the earth from the saints:

- Worship and Prayer is not primarily about changing God's mind or course of action on matters on the earth-as God does not change his mind. Instead, worship and prayer is more about getting ourselves aligned with God's heart on certain matters; so that when God does what he had already predetermined what He was going to do, we have understanding of why God did it so as not to be offended with God.

- Intimacy with God through worship and prayer is meant to give us the "oil" of joy (Matthew 25:1-10). It is important to have an internal source of joy that cannot be taken away- BUT the real action is in mobilizing people, and handling physical/material resources in obedience to God.

- The importance of violent intercession with fasting, and extravagant acts of worship is minimized- such radical acts of devotion cannot change God's mind and course of action on a matters related to earth. God was already going to do a certain miracle or not do it-regardless of how people respond with repentance, worship, and intercession.

At first it seems humble- that we are submitted to God's sovereign leadership. However, the practical consequence is this: *If I am filled with a satisfactory level of joy in my life, why should I spend time a lot of time in prayer (especially in intercession for the sake of others) when the real action is all about mobilizing people, influencing people, and handling physical and material resources?*

Most of the Body of Christ comes to the same conclusion I would: Prayer is for the weak, broken, and oppressed. If I am not broken or oppressed, I simply need to "check in with God" every day to make sure things is good in our relationship. Spending time with God becomes a luxury instead of a necessity. After making sure that everything is good with God, then its time to go out to where the real "action" is in the physical material realm. After all, this is how to really bring glory to Jesus anyway.

This is in contrast to the Hebraic view of relating to God in worship and prayer that is shared within many cultures:

- God is in heaven and we are on the earth. God has given people delegated authority on earth (Psalm 115:16; Genesis 1:26-27). We are also a governing body with Christ as our head in the heavenly realms.

- The heavenly realm (supernatural realm of angels and demons) interacts with the physical and material realm regularly with consistent patterns. While certain Biblical events and God's overall character do not change, God looks at how people respond on the earth to determine courses of action. In other words, the intensity of agreement with God on earth (i.e. through extravagant worship and giving, prayer and fasting, walking in humility with others etc.) influences how God responds to us on earth.

The Hebraic worldview like this puts an added emphasis on the importance of making effectual fervent intercession on behalf of people in word and in deeds:

- It means that we have a real important say (through prayer, fasting, and worship to Jesus) in whether God intervenes on the earth on behalf of His people-and how deeply God intervenes on our behalf. The depth of our agreement with Heaven's desires for us beat makes a significant difference on the earth.

- The heavenly realm interacts with the physical material realm regularly with consistent patterns. We had better understand from the Bible what those regular and consistent patterns are.

- It means that worship and prayer is about getting ourselves into alignment with God's heart (getting the oil of intimacy in Matthew 25:1-10) AND inviting God to affect the realm of angels and demons to change what will happen on the earth.

- The importance of anointed intercession with fasting and extravagant worship with offerings to God cannot be ignored or minimized. It means that the real action is in that deep place of communion and intimacy with God-just as much as influencing people and working with physical and material resources.

At first this worldview seems extremely arrogant- it's as if we can interact with God a personal way and that it really matters in the affairs on the earth.

In reality, this worldview reality is about God- He actually wants to directly interact with people like you and me. In fact scripture says that there are three types of people that God will directly seek out: worshippers who worship in spirit and truth (John 4:23-24), intercessors who will stand in the gap for the sake of others and plead for mercy (Ezekiel 22:30), and those who are whole-heartedly committed to Him (2 Chronicles 16:9). That God Almighty would condescend so deeply- that we could directly communicate with Jesus should tell us about how much we are worth to our God.

PART II:

A GLOBAL IDENTITY CRISIS

4

WHO DO YOU SAY I AM?

"Now this is eternal life: that they may know you, the only true God, and Jesus Christ, whom you have sent." – John 17:3.

Most personal spiritual warfare (including deliverance from demonic influences) centers around understanding our identity in Christ and the practical implications for our lives. We gain our identity from whoever (or whatever) we believe is our source of physical provision, our sense of significance, joy, affection, and vision from. *Who am I? Where did I come from? Why am I here?* These are common identity questions we must all face.

Understanding our identity is critical to winning personal battles with the enemy, winning corporate battles for the sake of our communities, and then finally driving satan's influence off the planet forever. If our identity is eternally secure in our extraordinary God who is humble, the result will be extraordinary humility. Extraordinary humility releases the power of God in extraordinary ways to overcome satan's best invisible fortresses of darkness. James tells us that God gives grace to the humble. Satan understands this threat and has attacked this generation related to identity like never before.

A whole generation is suffering from an identity crisis. A whole generation is posting their "great exploits" on *you tube* in hopes that their video will go viral resulting in fame and fortune. We have lost an understanding of who Jesus is. When someone tries to give our nation a reminder, they are branded as "narrow minded", "bigoted", or "homophobic". On any given weekend when I go out evangelizing and I bring up Jesus, I get a ton of interesting answers.

It reminds me of what was happening in the time of Jesus in the midst of a culture that supposedly knew the Messiah was coming:

When Jesus came to the region of Caesarea, Philippi, he asked his disciples, "Who do you say the Son of Man is?"
They replied, "Some say John the Baptist; others say Elijah; and still others, Jeremiah or one of the prophets."
"But what about you?" he asked. "Who do you say I am?"
(Matthew 16:13-15)

Of course, we know the rest of the story- Peter gave the right answer and in turn, Jesus shared with Peter what his identity in Christ is. Out of that understanding of the identity of God we will find our own identity. It is out of this firm foundation that Jesus would build his church and prevail against satan and his demonic hordes.

Of course, Peter (like all of us) did not really get what Jesus was saying. Peter still didn't understand the implications of who Jesus is. When Jesus talked about suffering and death, Peter didn't get it to the point where he got one of the worst rebukes in all of scripture. The disciples still had problems with visions of their own grandeur at the expense of other people. It was only a chapter later that they finally began to understand at the heart level- and they didn't like it at all. Unfortunately, I can relate all too well.

On a Friday in the midst of the December 2006 Global Bridegroom Fast, suddenly the Spirit of God fell upon me. In the midst of the fasting, God spoke to me of His plans for me concerning the year 2007 and beyond. It was a warning concerning the need for great humility. The prophecy concluded with the phrase, *"Who you are to Me is more important than anything you can do for Me."*

The year 2007 was an incredible year of spiritual adventure, anointed prayer and fasting, fruitfulness, and impact. I suddenly found myself in a leadership role on the cutting edge of the bringing together of missions and prayer under the leadership of Jesus. God released astounding answers to prayer in Taiwan, South Korea, Tajikistan, Israel, Venezuela, Egypt, Turkey, the United States, and other nations. As a prayer leader on a worship team, people were regularly getting healed in the prayer meetings as we experimented with combining worship and prayer in multiple languages in one meeting.

Suddenly in 2008 the season switched, producing an identity crisis. The leadership role ended. People were suddenly upset at me and I did not know why at the time. Worst of all, the incredible anointing for prayer was suddenly gone and I had gotten some bad teaching related to what losing "the kingly anointing" meant. The God I knew was suddenly not relating to me in ways I knew- giving me direct questions of who God is. Without knowing who God is, how was I supposed to know who I am? Who was this God anyway? God was about to reveal Himself in the midst of the chaos.

Jesus as the Master of Breakthroughs

In the midst of the confusion, God released two rather remarkable encounters to me because of their timing. On July 16th, 2008 (my 18th spiritual birthday), the IHOP-KC community was in the midst of yet another season of fasting and prayer. God had spoken to the leadership team about "wrapping the mantle of His name around our face" related to Exodus 33:19 through Exodus 34:7. A horrific cyclone had just hit Myanmar and over 100,000 people were dead. Over 1 million more were in danger of dying.

Feeling rather oppressed, I went early that morning to get some prayer from the healing rooms. In the midst of prayer, the fear of the Lord came upon me. This would be the last day to fast for me as I had obligations in Minneapolis. One of my friends and ministry partners had passed on to be with Jesus.

Later that morning in the midst of a normal worship with the word prayer meeting- the presence and glory of God simply broke into the room and people rose to their feet, hands raised to heaven in worship. Some in the room fell upon their faces. Jesus, the Master of Breakthroughs, had entered the room. It was later that day in the midst of a men's fasting team led by Allen Hood that we would learn that there was spiritual breakthrough with the Myanmar Dictatorship government to allow aid into the nation through Daniel and Levi Lim.

Jesus as Faithful and True and healer-

Several weeks later on my natural birthday, I was again in the prayer room- and I was still heart-broken and confused. An outbreak of the Holy Spirit in Lakeland Florida initiated in April had been growing in strength as many were experiencing remarkable healings. Excitement was building that perhaps, this was the beginning of another great awakening in America. There were reports of resurrections from the dead. Suddenly, the outpouring of the Holy Spirit abruptly ended as yet another high-profile leader was publicly exposed in scandalous sin.

Across many of the charismatic streams in the Body of Christ, many were wounded and confused. Carrying some of the burden about this, I went into a side-room prayer meeting dedicated to praying in tongues together. In the midst of praying in the Holy

Spirit, several people began weeping and wailing as if in travail. I dropped to my knees as I had a vision:

I saw Jesus come to me. He had long, black wavy hair. He was dressed in radiant garments. His eyes were a flame of fire. Yet his eyes/cheeks reflected an endless depth of tenderness and compassion. In his nail scarred hands he held a sash that was golden and glistening, but wrinkled and looking dirty. On it was written, "Jehovah Rapha" in crimson letters.

Jesus then asked me, *"Is there anyone I can entrust this to?"* Tears were streaking down His cheeks.

I said, "I'm not worthy."

Jesus then said, *"I didn't ask you whether you were worthy. I asked, 'Is there anyone I could entrust this to?'"*

He paused and stared straight into my eyes- more tears fell from his eyes and said, *"Can I entrust this to YOU?"*

The grief I felt was so intense. I got down on my face before the LORD crying out, "I wish you could trust me with this; I wish you could trust me with this." It was not primarily about the power and authority to heal. *It was all about comforting the heart of King Jesus.*

As I reflect on this encounter, Paul wrote in 1 Corinthians 4 that anyone who is given a trust from God must be proven faithful. However, we cannot be faithful and trustworthy in the midst of very difficult situations unless we deeply know the faithfulness and trustworthiness of Jesus (even when we don't like the difficult circumstances He could easily deliver us from-but is not doing).

The Armor of God- what was Paul really talking about?

Acts 19 records the Apostle Paul's ministry in Ephesus, a city steeped in idolatry and sorcery. God released extraordinary miracles through the Apostle Paul and the ministry team-so much that it shook the whole city. The invisible spiritual clash in the heavenly places produced both a riot and a revival. Aware of the invisible war, Paul wrote to the Ephesians:

Finally, be strong in the LORD and in his mighty power. Put on the full armor of God so that you can take your stand against the devil's schemes. For our struggle is not against flesh and blood, but against the rulers, against the authorities, against the powers of this dark world and against the spiritual forces of evil in the heavenly realms. Therefore, put on the full armor of God, so that when the day of evil comes, you may be able to stand your ground, and after you have done everything, to stand. Stand firm then, with the belt of truth buckled around your waist, with the breastplate of righteousness in place, and with your feet fitted with the readiness that comes from the

42

gospel of peace. In addition to all this, take up the shield of faith, with which you can extinguish all the flaming arrows of the evil one. Take the helmet of salvation and the sword of the Spirit, which is the word of God. And pray in the Spirit on all occasions with all kinds of prayers and requests. With this in mind, be alert and always keep on praying for all the saints. (Ephesians 6:10-18)

We look at the armor of God and make Christian children's posters about it-but do we really understand what Paul was saying in this passage?

Keep in mind that this was the same Apostle Paul who wrote to the Church in Philippi related to ambition. Paul shared his:

I want to know Christ and the power of his resurrection and the fellowship of sharing in his sufferings, becoming like him in his death, and so somehow to attain to the resurrection from the dead (Philippians 3:10-11).

If the center of Paul's ambition was to know Jesus, yet he was also advocating putting on "the armor of God" he must be referring to Jesus Christ himself.

Putting on the belt of truth is more than simply knowing the right information or even right morals. Truth is a person- Jesus Christ is Faithful and True. Everything stands upon the Truth of who Jesus is. Do we know Jesus' faithfulness towards us? Are we able to perceive the faithfulness of Jesus when circumstances (and the flaming arrows of the enemy) would suggest otherwise?

Putting on the breast plate of righteousness speaks of understanding your legal position before God through Christ Jesus- *and how God feels about us.* Nothing shuts down the human heart faster than shame and condemnation-yet it is a common tactic of the enemy. Jesus Christ is our righteousness- the One who is pure took upon Himself our guilt to make atonement for us. Understanding that God still enjoys us in the midst of our immaturity, brokenness, and frustration with ourselves (because we just blew it and sinned) gives us confidence to run to God and not away from Him.

Jesus Christ is the Prince of Peace. Putting our feet in the Gospel of peace represents putting all of our ambitions into simply loving Jesus and His people. God knows our deepest desires and knows how to fulfill them perfectly. Without the peace of Jesus, we end up running into fear and selfish ambition that makes us an easy target for the enemy. God also warned that He will shake everything that can be shaken (Hebrews 12:26-29). Are we at peace in

Christ? It can produce gratitude in even the most difficult of situations. Jesus said that the peace-makers are greatly blessed by God.

Jesus is the Author and Finisher of our faith (Hebrews 12:1-3). We can look at the overall narrative of the Bible to see the faithfulness of God in contrast to the unfaithfulness of man. Paul understood that if Jesus began a good story on a global level and has finished it- He will finish the story he is writing in us. One of the enemy's favorite "fiery arrows" to use against us is that of discouragement when the story of our lives takes an unexpected (and usually rather unfavorable) twist. By taking up the shield of faith- we become impossible to discourage.

Spiritual warfare begins with a battle over truth. In our battle for truth- we do not keep the truth to ourselves, but we use the truth on behalf of other people. We are to take up the "sword of the Spirit"-not to hack people up, but to set people free.

Using the Sword of the Spirit to tearing down lies about God.

On the individual level of spiritual warfare, the battle is about knowing God at the heart level. In the midst of our fight with the enemy we have not been left defenseless. Paul wrote,

For though we live in the world, we do not wage war as the world does. The weapons we fight with are not the weapons of the world. On the contrary, they have divine power to demolish strongholds. We demolish arguments and every pretension that sets itself up against the knowledge of God, and we take captive every thought to make it obedient to Christ. And we will be ready to punish ever act of disobedience, once your obedience is complete. (2 Corinthians 10:3-6)

Even as darkness flees in the presence of light, truth is much more powerful than deception.

The problem is that often our souls (our emotions and our patterns of thinking etc.) are often chained to deception that attracts demonic activity and oppression. Usually beginning with a very negative event miss-interpreted or a pattern of sin, the enemy tries to gain a foothold. Over time, satan and the demonic forces of wickedness can build a cluster of lies into a stronghold in the minds and emotions of people to oppress them.

In biblical times, a stronghold was a place of refuge for human activity- it both kept people safe within and the enemy was kept outside. Cities were built upon hills as fortified strongholds and became the centers of near-east society in biblical times. The psalmist talks about God being our stronghold and refuge. In building the Kingdom of God, we are building strongholds of righteousness that repel the tactics of the enemy by equipping and training people.

In the same way, demonic strongholds both keep the truth of Jesus out and provide a sheltered place for sin or demonic activity to grow, relatively un-resisted. Once the first stronghold is built, it is much easier for satan to build another one in the hearts of people. The enemy's end goal is that a believer would renounce their faith or at-least neutralize them from effectively building the Kingdom of God.

The problem with strongholds of darkness is they repel light and truth related to knowing Jesus at the heart-level. However, we have the power through scripture to break them:

For the word of God is living and active. Sharper than a double-edged sword, it penetrates even to dividing soul and spirit, bone and marrow; it judges the thoughts and attitudes of the heart. (Hebrews 4:12)

Strongholds that promote demonic activity are chained to wounding in our soul (emotional memories, patterns of thinking etc.). It takes skillful use of the word of God under the anointing of the Holy Spirit to break a stronghold without further injuring the person's soul.

Once the enemy is exposed and kicked out, healing and re-establishing the practice of truth is essential. (Otherwise, the enemy can make use of the wounding to build a new, more powerful stronghold.) It is now time to build a stronghold of Truth backed up with action related to who Jesus is and who we are to Him.

Who is our Source at the End of the Age? Jesus as Bridegroom, King, and Judge

As we draw closer to the last battles at the end of the age, it is clear that the Holy Spirit is presenting Jesus in deeper ways, previously veiled to other generations. The Kingship of Jesus is perhaps the most-well known. Jesus is King with power over the heavens and the earth. In His great wisdom, He is leading all of human history to a glorious and terrible climax. Satan and his demonic hordes cannot stop Him. We get to choose whether we will be for Him or against Him.

However, what often gets forgotten is the personal dimension of the Kingship of Jesus. Not only is Jesus King, but He is kind and good. His leadership for our lives is perfect- for those who love Him. Everything Jesus said, He intends to fulfill it. However, we must come into agreement with His leadership in word and deed for all of the good intentions to be fulfilled in our lives.

Jesus is not just a King- He is a *Bridegroom King*. Jesus compares Himself to a Jealous Husband to His people in the Hebraic scriptures. God is not passive, but infinitely passionate towards people. Even small acts of obedience and humility are cherished by God forever. Even as a Bridegroom and Bride mutually enjoy each other at the wedding, God is raising up a company of people who enjoy God deeply as they experience the enjoyment of God over their hearts and lives. Through anointed teaching on this subject through Mike Bickle, John Piper, and others- and the demonstration of God's activity through films such as *Furious Love* and *Father of Lights* a whole generation has greater access than ever to understand His emotions towards us.

God promised that there would be a generation where everyone could prophesy associated with the outpouring of His Spirit. This is the generation that will not just prophesy related to what God is doing- but it is a generation that will understand the emotional "why" in the heart of God and call people to the eternal wedding feast. There will be a remnant that will bring the heart of God great joy in the midst of great anguish.

God will also highlight Jesus as Judge to this generation. God is looking to make His manifold wisdom known to powers and principalities in the heavenly realm through the saints. The name Daniel literally means "God is my Judge". The Bible deliberately does not mention Daniel's sin but focuses on the wisdom of God. When God's wisdom is proven to be supreme (under the most extreme circumstances), God executes judgment in the midst of principalities and powers resulting in dramatic shifts on the earth in the affairs of men.

Jesus is the eternal Judge of all people. Scripture is clear that all will stand before him for evaluation. However, not much has been spoken related to eternal judgment of the righteous or the wicked. Without an understanding of eternal judgment, our perspective becomes very near-sighted and focused on the next 70 years instead of the next 1 million years.

This generation needs to understand that any acts of wisdom and humility will affect eternity. Without an eternal perspective, we will lose hope as wickedness increases on the earth. Without an understanding of eternal judgment, the danger of eternal punishment, and the prize of eternal rewards, this generation will not rise up in courageous humility, wisdom, and unending love to overcome the wickedness in this age.

5

WHO AM I TO GOD?

Our generation is in the midst of an identity crisis. One of the primary issues of spiritual warfare is "identity theft" in this generation. Satan and his demonic kingdom have specialized in challenging this generation related to our identity in scripture. A million different voices are attempting to define our identity related to selling their products or ideas. Marketers and other cultural influencers have learned, *if you can define and shape identity, you can influence the values and choices of a generation.*

Our nation has forgotten who the God of Abraham, Isaac, and Jacob is- and the implications for our own lives. Only God himself can bestow and shape our true identity upon our lives. Yet since our nation has forgotten God, it opened up a huge identity void in the hearts of a generation searching for meaning and significance. As the result, we have been building a virtual "tower of Babel" related to social media:

"Come let us build ourselves a city, with a tower that reaches to the heavens, so that we may make a name for ourselves and not be scattered over the face of the whole earth."
(Genesis 11:4)

Instead of building a city of brick and mortar, we are building a "virtual city" with silicon and fiber optic cables. This "virtual world" has caused narcissism and entitlement in our society to explode. (I'm guessing this statement will not get many "likes".) In the midst of the sea of information and ideas, there has never been so much moral confusion and chaos.

The IHOPU student awakening in 2009:

The International House of Prayer had just turned 10 years old and we were praying for revival to break out. Our prayers got more intense as mainline denomination after denomination within the Body of Christ changed the clear teaching of the Bible related to sexuality and the problem of sexual immorality in 2009. The economy was suffering under "the great recession". The pressure and the heartache pushed many to press into God with more intense prayer and combine it with fasting.

Prophetic people had received dreams and visions of a season of renewal and awakening coming to the IHOP-KC community. Beginning at the end of October, Jesus began "tipping" the bowls of intercession and giving hints to our community of a coming visitation of refreshing as the manifest presence began coming into some of the "behind the scenes" meetings.

On a Wednesday morning, Wes Hall's class gathered in the main FCF auditorium for morning worship before the teaching time. Yet something was clearly different this morning- students who did not drink, were laughing with joy as if "drunk on wine" at 9am in the morning. This childish behavior was not stopping as the teaching began. To deal with this "distraction", Wes called the worship leader back on stage to do worship- exalting Jesus would quickly douse any foolishness of mere human (or demonic) activity.

Of course corporately worshipping Jesus when the Holy Spirit is manifesting in power is the equivalent to putting gasoline on the fire. Instead of stopping the "distraction", the laughter, weeping, shaking, and other manifestations increased- and began spreading throughout the whole class. By this time, other classes in session began filing into the main auditorium- and were not leaving. Texts messages began flooding the mission base: *"It's happening!"* By evening, FCF was packed with people and the manifest presence of God. The date was November 11th, 2009.

Thus began a season of roughly 10 months of special IHOPU student awakening meetings at IHOP-KC. The IHOPU student awakening was broadcasted live through the internet and GOD-TV, bringing an "ankle deep" taste of renewal and revival to many college campuses, universities, homes, and even places around the world where it is illegal to preach the gospel.

In the midst of the IHOPU student awakening, the Holy Spirit was emphasizing two primary activities: First, many IHOPU students and staff were set free of besetting sins related to self-hatred. Many testified to feeling God's love towards them and knowing their value to Jesus for the very first time. Strongholds of rejection and bitterness crumbled as the Holy Spirit brought truth into broken hearts. Student after student got up and testified of getting set free of immorality, eating disorders, and alcoholism. Depression and suicide were broken off. Families were restored, physical bodies were healed, and boldness imparted to share the love of Jesus that they had been experiencing with other people. Over 5,000 testimonies came in related to inner healing, the breaking of strongholds, and physical healing during the IHOPU student awakening.

The second primary emphasis was on the importance of water baptism. Jesus commanded that those who turned to Him in repentance would be water baptized (Mark 16:16; Matthew 28:19) as a public sign of internal saving faith. Over 1,000 people were publicly water baptized for the first time in the midst of the IHOPU student awakening. Many testified of getting set free of brokenness, sin, and bondage in the midst of water baptism.

The power (and controversy) of water baptism:
Historically, water baptism has been one of the greatest controversies affecting the Body of Christ-even to the point of causing bloodshed. Why? Water baptism is publicly, symbolically, and firmly choosing to identify with the victory Jesus- in front of demonic principalities and powers. Water baptism is about our core identity in Jesus Christ. Satan understands the "in your face" statement behind water baptism and has introduced confusion over the subject.

Jesus commanded his disciples to be water baptized. Paul went on to explain the significance of this prophetic act:

What shall we say, then? Shall we go on sinning so that grace may increase? By no means! We died to sin; how can we live in it any longer? Or don't you know that all of us where were baptized into Christ Jesus were baptized into his death? We were therefore buried with him through baptism into death in order that, just as Christ was raised from the dead through the glory of the Father, we too may live a new life (Romans 6:1-4).

In him (Christ), *you were also circumcised, in the putting off of the sinful nature, not with a circumcision done by the hands of men but with circumcision done by Christ, having been buried with him in baptism and raised with him through your faith in the power of God, who raised him from the dead. (Colossians 2:11-12)*

The power behind water baptism is in physically identifying with the death, burial, and resurrection of Jesus Christ. Water baptism is a clear sign of active, saving faith- as faith without works is dead.

The power of willful identification cannot be under-estimated. In many cultures, people can freely believe anything-as long as they don't do anything about it. For example in India, someone can freely receive Jesus Christ as God, do good things, and even do miracles and the Hindu-dominated culture is happy with that. The same is true in Buddhism and Islam- someone can freely believe in Jesus Christ without social or economic penalty.

However, should they decide to be water-baptized, (a public declaration they are renouncing all other gods and identifying only with Jesus Christ), the persecution begins. In Saudi Arabia, it is considered to be the crime of apostasy, punishable by death. In Orthodox Judaism, if a member of the community turns to Jesus, the whole community has a public funeral for them. In Hinduism and Buddhist communities, often the whole family will disown a baptized follower of Jesus since they disowned their family gods (and the demons behind them).

Baptism raises the question of who are we going to identify with by our own, free choices? At the end of the age, the antichrist will require his worshippers to take an economic mark upon their right hand or forehead. It is a mark of identification with worshipping the beast. Someone doesn't "accidentally" take the mark (or wake up and find their roommates have tattooed a number on their forehead as a prank) and eternally lose their salvation at the end of the age. It will take proven loyalty to the Antichrist and his agenda to gain this "mark of (dis)honor".

Consequently, while Jesus loves the little children and wants all to come to him, He cannot (and will not) make the choice for them. Everyone, whether young or old, must make a decisive choice to consistently identify with Jesus through water baptism. In streams of the Body of Christ that practice infant water baptism, there is a significant problem: They are robbing a generation of the opportunity to personally and publicly identify with Jesus in the most direct, symbolic, and biblically prescribed way.

If the Church practices infant baptism, the kingdom of darkness often promotes a lie into the hearts of people: *"I'm good to go to heaven simply because my parents baptized me when I was a baby."* For many, infant baptism turns into a "license to sin" out of presumption that they are automatically forgiven. In many nations where the institutional church practices infant baptism the people still practice syncretism-where they actively worship false gods, while believing infant baptism is their ticket to heaven. This lie also directly hinders people from understanding that they must personally turn from sin and follow Jesus for their salvation.

Truly understanding our identity in Christ will produce humility

Underlying the issue of baptism and many issues besetting sin is the issue of identity. At the end of the age, the Holy Spirit is going to emphasize our individual identity as being sons and daughters of God, with access to the King. The Holy Spirit is also going to emphasize that we are His workmanship- or story. Not only is God going to finish the story on a grand-scale, God will finish our story on the individual, human level in grand fashion as well.

God is also going to emphasize to emphasize our individual identity as the Bride of Christ and friends of the Bridegroom-with access to the deep emotional things of God. There is nothing quite like the pleasure of knowing the deep things of God. John the Baptist had heard the voice of the Bridegroom and his joy was complete. With his identity secure in Christ, he was free to do whatever it took so that the Bridegroom could have the Bride-including getting out of the way for the next phase of God's redemptive plan.

This initial outpouring of the Holy Spirit at IHOP-KC was not unexpected. On a number of occasions, Mike Bickle told a prophetic story from 1984. In essence, Mike Bickle and Bob Jones had a prophetic experience related to asking God for the release prophetic promises related to a national great awakening in America that would touch the ends of the earth. They had a prophetic encounter related to Joseph, the baker, and the cup-bearer.

The main point of the prophetic message was that God was going to require great humility in the days ahead. He warned that those who did not produce humility would lose their ministries (just as the baker lost his head in the story of Joseph). Meanwhile, those who did produce humility would be exalted to serve wine in the presence of the King (just as the cupbearer was). It was also a statement that God would begin this process in 10 years[1].

Ten years later in 1994, the "wine" of the Holy Spirit was poured out in Toronto under Pastor John Arnott. As people were touched by the supernatural, they would react with weeping, seemingly uncontrollable laughter, shaking, "crunching", and falling to the floor.

During the IHOPU student awakening the same things happened. Underlying both outpourings of the Spirit, God was healing the broken-hearted and giving experience of their identity in Christ according to the Bible. In the midst of the chaotic nature of the awakening meetings, God was sharing in personal ways how valuable each and every one of His children are to Him. He was answering the prayer that we would be "rooted and grounded" in the love of God.

Understanding our identity in Christ *must* produce humility-otherwise, we don't understand who Jesus is or our identity in

---

[1] Encounter Jesus series part 4. used by permission http://mikebickle.org/faq/

Christ. Paul talked much about humility in Philippians 2 and we often uses Jesus as the example of humility in verses 5-8. However, the key verse is actually much earlier:

If you have any encouragement, from being united in Christ, if any comfort from his love, if any fellowship with the Spirit, if any tenderness and compassion, then make my joy complete by being like-minded, having the same love, being one in spirit and purpose. (Philippians 2:1-2)

It is relatively easy to walk in humility, serve others, and bless others *if our identity does not feel threatened.* However, if our source of physical provision, security, joy, sense of significance, or vision feels threatened we tend to lash out in selfish ambition or vain conceit as children. As adults, our actions tend to be more refined with subtle manipulation or gossip but the root issues remain the same.

In the midst of the IHOPU student awakening, God gave plenty of opportunity for offense. Many were offended at who God chose to lead it (Wes Hall, Allen Hood, etc.). Those on the platform had opportunities to be offended at how others responded to their leadership. Others were offended at the strange behavior of people- and dismissed it. Still others had wrapped their identity around getting touched and the opportunities flowing from the renewal meetings (different than being rooted in Jesus himself). The demonic realm attempted to exploit all of these frustrations and many others.

The Example of Jesus:

So why is the understanding of our identity in God so important to humility and spiritual warfare? To answer this question, we simply need to look at Jesus Christ as a man. Philippians 2 tells us that he laid aside his "divine rights" and walked on earth like any other human being did. The Apostle John gives us more insight:

It was just before the Passover Feast. Jesus knew that the time had come for him to leave this world and go to the Father. Having loved his own who were in the world, he now showed them the full extent of his love. The evening meal was being served and the devil had already prompted Judas Iscariot, son of Simon to betray Jesus. Jesus knew that the Father had put all things under his power, and that he had come from God and was returning to God. (John 13:1-3)

It was out of this eternal well of identity that Jesus walked out humility and love to the uttermost in the next 10 chapters of John, beginning with washing the feet of his disciples who were fickle and in one case, fake.

Years earlier, Jesus confronted satan in the wilderness by the power of the Holy Spirit. The battle actually started in Matthew 3 when Jesus came to John the Baptist desiring to be baptized. However, John the Baptist immediately recognized the holiness and humility in Jesus by the Holy Spirit and asked that Jesus would baptize him. In the invisible realm, God the Son was submitting to and honoring God the Holy Spirit (empowering John's ministry).

Matthew 3:16 describe what happens next: As soon as Jesus was baptized, he went up out of the water. At that moment heaven was opened, and he saw the Spirit of God descending like a dove and lighting on him. Not to take the glory and honor, the Holy Spirit quickly presents Jesus before the crowd. God the Holy Spirit comes upon the Jesus as a dove coming from heaven. Not to be outdone by the divine pleasure and joy taking place on earth, Heaven opens and God the Father joins in. Matthew 3:17 declares,

"And a voice from heaven said, 'This is my Son, whom I love; with him I am well pleased'."

In submitting to baptism of repentance, Jesus had honored the Father in his will. For the first time since He thundered the 10 commandments, the world hears the audible voice of Glory as the Father gives His thunderous approval of Jesus before all of Israel.

Following the dramatic events of the baptism of Jesus, scripture tells us Jesus was led into the wilderness. God was initiating the conflict with satan in Christ Jesus and Jesus fasted for 40 days.

The confrontation is recorded in Matthew 4:1-11. Two times, satan threw his best temptations beginning with, *"If you are the Son of God"*. The core of satan's attack was in the area of identity. In both of these cases, Jesus simply quoted the Word: *"It is written…!"*

In the midst of the first two temptations, satan remained hidden. However, since satan could not attack his identity in His Father, he went on to offer Him all the kingdoms of this world without the necessity of the cross. Simply an act of worship would do. Behind this temptation was a slanderous accusation against the source of His identity- His Father: *How could your Father require a noble man like you to go to the cross to win the kingdoms of the world?*

In the midst of this temptation satan exposed himself. Jesus' response was swift:

"Away from me Satan! For it is written: Worship the Lord your God, and serve him only." (Matthew 4:10).

Satan knew that if he could get Jesus to question His identity in His Father or the nature of His Father, the devil would succeed in ruining the plan of redemption for the human race. Jesus himself told his disciples that he had authority to call in the angels and end the plan.

If Jesus is truly King, where was the splendor and majesty worthy of a King? If Jesus is truly the Son of God, Where is the power to end the suffering of his loved ones (or to avoid that mess)? In the midst of the public humiliation, mental anguish, and physical agony at the cross, satan sneered at Jesus through the religious leaders and other passer-bys:

"You who are going to destroy the temple and build it in three days, save yourself! Come down from the cross, if you are Son of God. In the same way the chief priests, the teachers of the law and the elders mocked him. "He saved others," they said, "but he can't save himself. He's the King of Israel! Let him come down now from the cross, and we will believe in him." (Matthew 27:40-42)

Of course, we know that Jesus stayed on the cross- obedient unto death in the most horrid fashion and triumphant forever. Is not Jesus worthy?

6
WHO AM I BECOMING?
GROWING UP BY GRACE

"Sow a thought, reap an action; sow an action, reap a habit; sow a habit, reap a character; sow a character, reap a destiny."
- Stephen Covey

Before I knew Jesus, I was a cub scout in elementary school. We would meet weekly in a small group (called a "den" meeting) and work on fun activities that would earn badges. We would also work on fun projects at home and with each other. We would also gather for monthly "pack" meetings at the school and do larger group fun activities. In one particular month, we were to bake cakes and decorate them around the theme: *What do you want to be when you grow older?* There would be prizes for the best decorated cakes.

In grade school, I was incredibly gifted in playing chess- and I was beating most adults in chess. Naturally, I wanted to decorate the cake, "I want to be a professional chess player!" As we were preparing to bake and decorate the cake, my dear mother dropped the cake breaking the cake into pieces. Being a hard-headed, self-centered elementary school student, I threw a huge temper tantrum. My mom tried to make the best of the situation and said, "You could just frost the cake and write: *'I want to be a baker.'"* (Decades later, I wish I would have gone with my mom's suggestion- where at least I would have won a prize for funniest cake.)

As young kids, we grow up dreaming of being fire fighters, doctors, professional athletes, or perhaps President of the United States-something heroic. Then as we grow older, cruel worldly reality hits most of us in the face: *"It ain't gonna happen."* Broken-hearted and perhaps disillusioned, we settle for something less that is workable and practical. Unfortunately this is often how we approach our walk with Jesus as well.

So what do you want to be when you grow up? Most of us don't think much about the question of living in eternity with Jesus. Yet scripture indicates that understanding and then walking towards our future eternal destiny in Christ Jesus is a critical part of understanding our identity in Christ.

The judgment seat of Christ-is it going to be worth it? .

Looking unto Jesus, we see that he humbled himself to the uttermost as described in Philippians 2. Indeed, God has revealed that He is going to exalt Jesus as ruler over the heavenly realms and the earth where everyone will bow before Him. Before the Father, Jesus as a human being has proven that He is worthy to rule the earth forever. One day, a remnant from every tongue, tribe and ethnic group will declare their agreement with Heaven that Jesus is worthy to rule the earth forever.

However, related to us, Paul wrote extensively that all of us who love Jesus and have chosen Him will stand before Him at the judgment seat of Christ and give an account for our days upon the earth. Paul warned:

For we must all appear before the judgment seat of Christ, that each one may receive what is due him for the things done while in the body, whether good or bad. (2 Corinthians 5:10)

God intended for us that this final day would be one of great rejoicing in Jesus. However, for many in the Body of Christ, there won't be much to rejoice over because so much time, money, and physical effort was simply wasted.

In Revelation 2 and 3, Jesus gave seven different messages to the Church in seven different locations. He gave words of affirmation followed by words of correction to the Body of Christ in each of these geographic areas. No matter how severe the rebuke was, Jesus always closed with the promise of tremendous eternal rewards to those who would overcome and correct what was wrong.

While everyone in Christ will have eternal life in heaven, our experience of eternal life will greatly differ in terms of the capacity to experience the joy of the Lord, to bless other people and to fellowship with Jesus. While everyone will have the glory and honor of our position as God's beloved ones, the measure of eternal glory and honor in Christ that we have will differ greatly from one person to another. What is ignored on the earth but done in love will be highly esteemed in heaven. Jesus promised that He would not forget- even the cup of cold water given to bless in His name.

Even in His judgments, we will all be overwhelmed at his goodness towards us. We didn't earn any rewards- we simply took

58

what the power and resources that are already God's and simply loved Him with them. Paul wrote:

But by the grace of God I am what I am, and his grace to me was not without effect. No, I worked harder than all of them-yet not I, but the grace of God that was in me.
(1 Corinthians 15:10)

Meanwhile, God then rewards us with His joy over what we did to love Him as if it was all ours to begin with. Jesus is completely just, but in His kindness, He will reward our love far beyond anything we deserve.

What is so amazing about grace?
God as a wise creator has given us our physical beings. Like Adam, He has set us on the earth in our family. God has also given us as human beings, physical abilities (that were developed as we grew)-such as the ability to speak, the ability to walk, see, hear etc. God also gave us the ability to think, experience, evaluate things, and to then make choices. As human beings, God has also given us the ability to receive affection and love from others, while also giving it out in meaningful ways. In His wisdom, God gave some people more ability than others in all of these areas. None of us earned these basic abilities from the beginning of our existence. God in His grace gave us these abilities. Theologians call this *"common grace"*- the glory and honor God gives all human beings in His image to choose.
God revealed Himself to us as righteous, humble, and kind in Christ Jesus. He fought for us against sin, death, and eternal condemnation when we could not fight for ourselves-and won. When we gave our lives over to Jesus, He removed our identity as "sons of perdition" and gave us a new identity as "Children of God". God changed our whole future destiny from being "objects of wrath" to "citizens of heaven", destined to reign with Jesus forever. We simply chose to agree with Jesus- what He did for us and what he is asking us to do by the power he gives us. We did absolutely nothing on our own to merit God's favor upon us- it was all by the grace of God.
Bible teachers call this dimension of grace *"saving grace"*. Paul gave a detailed explanation of God's saving grace to us in Romans 3-8. God saved us from *the eternal consequences of sin* in changing our identity in Christ Jesus because we believed. God is saving us from the *law of sin* (the downward progressive spiral of sin leading to eternal destruction) by progressively renewing our mind, emotions, and changing the way we make decisions. God will

then save us from the *presence of sin* by giving us a new body and by making all of creation new.

In the last two chapters, I have emphasized our new identity in Christ Jesus. The solution to our identity crisis as a generation is to first know who God is. Scripture gives us insight into the character, the nature of God. I highlighted Jesus as Bridegroom, King, and Judge. I also spent some time on Jesus as the Master of Breakthroughs and Jesus as Faithful and True. The armor of God in spiritual warfare speaks of Jesus as the Author and Finisher of our faith; our source of peace, our righteousness, our salvation, and so much more.

The second part to solving the identity crisis is that we need to know how valuable we are to God. Scripture calls us individually the, sons of the Most High God, citizens of heaven, and living stones. We are also the Bride of Christ, God's holy temple and the Body of Christ. Using the example of Jesus, a correct understanding of our identity before God in Christ will produce active humility as Paul described in Philippians 2. If the long-term fruit of our understanding identity in Jesus Christ is not consistent with the growing nature of Jesus being formed in us, can we be sure that we are "in Christ"?

Empowering grace: We must continue to agree with God-but God will help us!

When we first made a choice to follow Jesus, we demonstrated our agreement by using the "common grace" God gives all human beings: We made a choice to follow Jesus and turn away from sin. At that moment, the Holy Spirit came to dwell within our human spirit and made us clean. However, our physical bodies and souls are still subject to the *law of sin* -the tendency for our sin grow progressively more damaging to ourselves and others, and end in death and eternal destruction (see Romans 1:18-32; James 1:15-17; Genesis 3-6).

We were powerless to save ourselves from the *eternal consequences of sin* through human effort. While we can restrain our behavior, we are still powerless in our own self-will and human strength to overcome *the law of sin.* Paul rebuked the Church in Galatia for relying on human ritual and self-will to overcome sin instead of the power of the Holy Spirit.

Numerous New Testament passages warn that those who intentionally practice sin will not inherit the Kingdom of God (regardless of whether they prayed a prayer or not). Thus, our freedom from the eternal consequences of sin will be short-lived unless God continues to do something to keep us in agreement with Him. Paul wrote about this horrible predicament:

What a wretched man I am! Who will rescue me from this body of death? Thanks be to God-through Jesus Christ our Lord! So then, I myself in my mind am a slave to God's law, but in the sinful nature a slave to the law of sin. (Romans 7:24-25).

Thank God that this is not the end of the story. Paul continues:

Therefore, there is now no condemnation for those who are in Christ Jesus, because through Christ Jesus the law of the Spirit of life set me free from the law of sin and death. (Romans 8:1)

Even in our struggle against sin (sometimes successfully, sometimes not), we can still be completely secure in Christ through depending on the goodness of God through the Holy Spirit.

We all know about the law of gravity on earth. However, if you have ever flown in an airplane, you know that as the airplane engines roar to life the plane travels fast enough where it lifts off the ground and begins soaring to the heights. Once the plane is off the ground, the plane does not crash back to the earth, but continues to rise as the engines continue to run. The plane may hit turbulence, but the plane will still fly, thanks to the engines. Due to the powerful engines, the airplane defies the physical law of gravity. As long as the engines are on, the plane will not crash.

In the same way, the power of the Holy Spirit within our human spirit is far superior to the "law of sin" operating in our soul and our flesh. Without understanding anything and being in open rebellion against God, we unwittingly relied on the power of the Holy Spirit to convict us of our need of Jesus, and give us a new identity in Jesus.

Now that we have initially turned to agree with Jesus and love Him, we still need to rely on the Holy Spirit to empower us to overcome sin. We now get to choose how deeply we will depend on the Holy Spirit. The key to growing up into maturity in Christ is not "trying harder" but receiving more from "The Spirit of Grace". The apostle James tells us how:

But he gives us more grace. This is why Scripture says: "God opposes the proud, but gives grace to the humble." Submit yourselves, then to God. Resist the devil and he will flee from you. Come near to God and he will come near to you. Wash your hands, you sinners, and purify your hearts, you double minded. Grieve, mourn, and wail. Change your laughter to mourning and your joy to gloom. Humble yourselves before the Lord, and he will lift you up. (James 4:6-10)

The great news is that God is more excited to give us this empowering grace in the Holy Spirit than we are to receive it from His hand. My friend Paul Anderson said, "The key to holiness is not trying harder, but receiving more from God."

The current practical sin struggles today will not hold out forever if we continue to make practical choices to agree with Jesus. Even as the plane engines are far more powerful than the laws of gravity, the power of the Holy Spirit is far greater than the law of sin operating in our soul and human flesh.

Much of our individual spiritual warfare is about bringing down the enemy's lies about God imbedded deep within our emotions and experience so that we can receive more from God by the power of the Holy Spirit. When lies are broken in our soul, Grace and Truth can flood in bringing transformation in our emotions, thought patterns, and eventually our actions.

Empowering grace is not limited to simply overcoming personal patterns of sin. Through empowering grace, we can live together to see our communities experience transformation through a flood of God's glory. Through grace, God will even inspire some to confront and overcome principalities and powers over nations through extravagant devotion like in Daniel 9 and 10. This famous prophet spoke of a company who knew their God and would do great exploits by grace in the last days (Daniel 11:32).

Spiritual warfare over the grace message: Doctrines of demons.

Satan of course, knows this and wants to short-circuit the whole process. Satan's ultimate goal is to cause us to reject Jesus by willfully resisting the Holy Spirit in all areas of our life (willfully "turn the engine" completely off) so that our lives then crash back into the law of sin and the eternal consequences of sin. Paul warned of this in the last days:

The Spirit clearly says that in the later times some will abandon the faith and follow deceiving spirits and things taught by demons. Such teachings come through hypocritical liars, whose consciences have been seared as with a hot iron. (1 Timothy 4:1-2).

On each side of the path of life, there is a deep ditch to avoid: legalism (leading to condemnation when we fail or arrogance and entitlement if we succeed) or lawlessness (doing whatever sin we want in the name of "grace"). Even if satan cannot get us to ultimately reject Jesus, satan wants to minimize the eternal impact and glory in our lives.

Satan is greatly fearful of this generation. Perhaps this generation is called to partner with God to invite Jesus back to earth and bring about satan's demise. In our generation, the enemy has launched a major assault against the true grace message on several fronts in order to deceive God's people:

1. *An assault on the biblical doctrine of eternal hell: God's wrath against sin.* False teachers say that there is no eternal punishment (annhilationism), or that all religions go to the same place (universalism). Meanwhile the Bible warns about eternal wrath- for those outside of Jesus: God will give them what they "wanted" (the fullness of sin) and its consequences.

2. *The Babylonian false identity message* (with the name of Jesus slapped on it). The biblical identity message from Jesus will produce gratitude, humility, love, a desire for righteous words and actions, and ultimately great joy and peace. A false identity message (even one with 'in Christ') will produce arrogance, an "entitlement mentality", bitterness, and confidence to sin under the guise: "I deserve these (temporary) pleasures". It often leads to a false grace message.

3. *A false grace-confidence message* (with the name of Jesus slapped on it). This doctrine gives a false eternal security for believers to live in blatant compromise with sin (a form of rebellion against Jesus) without concern over the New Testament warnings of eternal loss. How can we "love Jesus" while at the same time completely reject His leadership? A true grace message inspires and empowers us into deeper agreement with Jesus. A false grace message gives confidence to rebel against Jesus into lawlessness.

4. *A false legalism message*- that we can earn our way to eternal life through self-will and human effort apart from God's grace offered through Jesus Christ. Most world religions teach some form of this message.

Standing by grace against the flood-tide of sexual immorality and other "false comforts"

Perhaps the number one threat facing a young generation is the subtle sequence of sin related to sexual immorality. The assault on the doctrine of grace is meant to drown a whole generation in immorality related sin and bring about a bitter disconnect with God.

Satan is after this generation to steal, kill, and destroy the inheritance of Jesus in us. In the same way, satan desires to steal the eternal rewards of love that Jesus wants to freely give us forever.

Sadly, a generation under 40 has been flooded with a culture of sexual immorality, drugs, and other sinful false comforts. Scripture calls any type of sexual activity outside of marriage sin. It grows to destroy our bodies and relationships. We are to submit ourselves to God as living sacrifices and honor God in our physical bodies. We know that demonic principalities and powers are working with evil men to create culture change where immorality is "normal", but why is a generation falling for it when God offers something so much better?

Sadly, the origins of our problems with immorality begin with our human self-centered pride. Our self-centered human pride is like natural gas in many ways. Natural gas is an odorless, colorless, tasteless gas that is potentially deadly. If it hits an ignition source, it explodes. Over the last few years, there have been some high-profile natural gas explosions where people died. In the same way, our human pride and selfishness is often undetectable until it "explodes" with spiritually destructive consequences for us and other people.

God in His goodness, allows us to detect the presence of eternally deadly self-centered human pride before destruction occurs. Gas companies add an inert chemical to natural gas to make it smell like rotten eggs. In the same way, God adds an acrid emotion so that we can detect deadly self-centered human pride: It can be detected through feelings of bitter envy or angry entitlement over being "mistreated"- in other words, bitterness and offense *before it explodes in outwardly destructive sinful actions.*

Bitterness is similar but a slightly different emotion than sorrow or feeling physical pain. Jesus cried out in pain and sorrow on the cross when He said, *"My God, My God, why have you forsaken me?"* Yet He was not bitter- having settled the issue in the Garden of Gethsemane.

When we are faced with this corrosive emotion that affects us physically, we are forced to make a choice: Do we fix the horrible physical and emotional feeling with a "sinful false comfort" such as sexual immorality, chemical abuse, or even "legitimate pleasures" in excess: a quick fix that satan offers, or do we turn away from our self-centered pride? Scripture is clear that human pride and bitterness is at the root of immorality.

"Now this was the sin of your sister Sodom: She and her daughters were arrogant, overfed, and unconcerned; they did

not help the poor and the needy. They were haughty and did detestable things before me. Therefore I did away with them as you have seen." (Ezekiel 16:49-50)

See to it that no one misses the grace of God and that no bitter root grows up to cause trouble and defile many. See that no one is sexually immoral, or is godless like Esau, who for a single meal sold his inheritance rights as the oldest son. (Hebrews 12:15-17)

The problem with a "quick fix" is that brings a false comfort, yet it has long-term negative consequences. It only hides the underlying problem of conceit and arrogance with its bitter poison allowing it to grow. Unless we repent of the whole structure of sin, it will completely destroy our walk with God, and other relationships. In the end, it leads to spiritual harlotry which God will condemn forever in Revelation 17.

However, a generation will arise who overcome by the empowering grace of the Holy Spirit. After the rewards have been handed out for everyone, we find them all singing a song of gratitude for His judgments:

And I saw what looked like a sea of glass mixed with fire and, standing beside the sea, those who had been victorious over the beast and his image and over the number of his name. They held harps given them by God and sang the song of Moses the servant of God and the song of the Lamb:

"Great and marvelous are your deeds, Lord God Almighty. Just and true are your ways, King of the Ages. Who will not fear you, O Lord, and bring glory to your name? For you alone are holy. All nations will come before you, for your righteous acts have been revealed."(Revelation 15:2-4)

All who are standing there know that none of them deserve ANYTHING they got from God's hand. However, in standing by grace they overcame and were victorious over the beast- the human sinful nature culminating in the Revelation 13 anti-Christ beast.

PART III:

SPIRITUAL AUTHORITY AND OVERCOMING WITCHCRAFT

7

EXERCISING OUR SPIRITUAL AUTHORITY IN CHRIST

Bible camp 1990

On the third evening of Bible Camp, the day's theme was *Real Power*. Greg, the main camp speaker spoke about the baptism of the Holy Spirit and the power of God available to us. After a closing prayer, he invited who so ever to get real with God related to the power of the Holy Spirit and get prayer. The previous night, one of the youth pastors prophesied that God was going to do some powerful things on this particular night.

As a one-day old follower of Jesus, I didn't know what I had gotten myself into. Who is the Holy Spirit? However, a voice internally was telling me to risk it all to be real with God. I also knew that after I gave my life to Jesus, something about baptism was important.

After praying that the Holy Spirit would come they asked everyone to hold out their arms to see if they were uneven. One lady came up who had a significant shoulder injury and one arm was literally several inches shorter than the other one. Not knowing what I was doing, I prayed something like, "Let her right arm grow to the same length as the other one in Jesus' name." Suddenly, her arm began to visibly grow in front of a group of 100 shocked teenagers, chaperones, and youth pastors from four different Lutheran youth groups.

God healed her arm and revival broke out. Other students experienced the baptism of the Holy Spirit, healing, and turning to know Jesus for the first time. The next year, Bible camp attendance tripled.

Beloved, this type of manifest spiritual authority is available to every genuine follower of Jesus- the first day they surrender to Christ. Jesus told his disciples:

"As you go, preach this message: 'The kingdom of heaven is near.' Heal the sick, raise the dead, cleanse those who have leprosy, drive out demons. Freely you have received, freely give." (Matthew 10:7-8)

Jesus later told his disciples (including all of us):

"Go into all the world and preach the good news to all creation. Whoever believes and is baptized will be saved, but whoever does not believe will be condemned. And these signs will accompany those who believe: In my name they will drive out demons; they will speak in new tongues; they will pick up snakes with their hands; and when they drink deadly poison, it will not hurt them at all; they will place their hands on sick people, and they will get well."
(Mark 16:15-18)

Yet, the experience of so many believers is that they pray in the name of Jesus and not much happens. This has caused many to question the authenticity of this passage of scripture. What's really going on here?

Understanding the relationship of delegated authority to power

In this instance and many others, God's servants operate under delegated authority. God has all authority and the power to do anything He says. However, it is rare for God to openly and *directly* intervene in human history in this age. Most of the time, God demonstrates power through angelic servants and through people who love him using His delegated authority.

Authority is not the same thing as power. For example, a police officer holds up his hand to stop traffic and the drivers stop their cars or trucks in obedience. A police officer does not have the physical ability to stop a car or a large semi-truck. If that police officer was wearing plain clothes like everyone else, and not showing the badge, I would not stop just because he wanted me to. The police officer does not have physical power to stop my vehicle.

On the other hand, if the police officer wearing the uniform raises his hand to stop traffic and I don't stop, he is backed up with the power of the state. He now has access to all of the resources of the state to physically cause me to stop. If it came to it, he could call out the police force with vehicles, guns, road blocks, traffic equipment, and even the entire military force of the state if necessary to cause me to stop-and then punish me for disobedience.

In the same way, we don't have power over satan and his demons. However, we do have delegated authority under Jesus within the boundaries described in the Bible. If the demonic kingdom disobeys our use of delegated authority within God-given righteous boundaries, God will back us up with the right to release all of the resources of heaven to use force to remove the demons and immediately punish them if they disobey:

For if God did not spare angels when they sinned, but sent them to hell putting them into gloomy dungeons to be held for judgment; (2 Peter 2:4)

You believe that there is one God. Good! Even demons believe that-and shudder. (James 2:19)

The devil and the demons in the kingdom of darkness are afraid of God's power backing up the use of our authority in Christ. Since demons would rather be free to roam the earth (and resist in that way) instead of chained in the pit until judgment day, they yield to us using the name of Jesus as we honor God's authority.

Spiritual authority based upon our identity in Christ

We all have legal authority to use the name of Jesus Christ because of who we are to God our Father. God the Father has given us the right to become children of God through Jesus Christ simply because we believe and love Him (John 1:12). Our legal authority in Christ is not based upon how well we are doing- it is based upon His loving affections over our lives.

For example, as a young child, I was constantly tormented by "monsters" in my dreams. I would always see monsters in my room and my heart was frozen in fear. I was also afraid of some of the rooms in my house as I could sometimes "see" monsters in the room. My parents would simply re-assure me and say, "Jess, it's only your imagination. Go back to bed." I would go back to bed and immediately feel that same fear. It traumatized me so badly that I was sometimes afraid to sleep in my bedroom.

It was after I had given my life to Jesus as a young teenager that I learned about what those "monsters" in my room were and how to get rid of them. Sometimes, I would still have scary dreams but I was no longer afraid. I would simply rebuke the demons in the name of Jesus and they were now scared of me. I learned about my spiritual authority in Christ early in my life and I would use it to pray for local church youth retreats and Bible camps. It was fun watching people get touched by God's goodness and them not knowing why it happened.

Many people in the body of Christ do not know what type of spiritual authority they have in Christ. As the result, the devil and his demonic cohorts get away with a lot of "illegal" activity in the lives of believers. In my senior year of college, my roommate was continuously tormented with fear. I would wake up with this young man tormented by demons. After rebuking them, my roommate would get relief. However, it wasn't until he learned how to use his spiritual authority in Christ *for himself* that the demonic realm left him alone.

Beloved, God has given *all* of us this authority in Jesus Christ. In the midst of using my spiritual authority as a youth, I still had *H-U-G-E* negative issues that God would need to firmly deal with related to bitterness, manipulation, and conceit among them. The point is that we can use our spiritual authority in Christ drive the enemy out of influencing our lives.

Authority in the name of Jesus is a privilege, and with delegated authority comes responsibility. No one on the earth exercises direct authority- From the president to the prisoner, we all exercise delegated authority over our lives. With delegated authority (and privilege) comes accountability. God gave Adam authority over the Garden of Eden. He did not own the garden, but he was allowed to enjoy and oversee it on God's behalf. However, Adam was also accountable to God for what happened in the garden- including keeping things in order (and not eating from that forbidden tree).

For example, I used to work with ACR homes, a company that puts special needs vulnerable adults into a residential setting. As staff, I had authority to use the house van to take residents out to eat or on rides. However, with the authority to use someone else's resources, I had to account for the use of that van to the residential supervisor. We would need to log in the date, where we went, the mileage, and any mechanical issues. We would also log in where we went and how our clients reacted in the residents' personal books. There were procedures in place in case we were involved in an accident.

In the same way, we have delegated authority in the name of Jesus Christ. Satan can no longer simply do whatever he wills because of our identity in Jesus Christ. However, we are accountable to Jesus in how we use our new found privilege and freedom. Do we use your freedom and the name of Jesus to simply advance our own selfish agenda or to advance the purposes of the Kingdom of God? Do we use our authority to build and bless other people? Do we neglect to use it (and let satan run amok, destroying lives)?

Exposing the Usurper

Jesus Christ won back for us the keys of death, hell, and the grave. Before we gave our lives to Jesus, we were slaves to sin. Yet now, the devil cannot force anyone in Christ do anything he wants. The enemy must get legal grounds from either God or us to continue his oppression. (As a good Father, why would He give legal permission for his adversary to mess with us unless like with Job or Peter, unless God already knows what is in us and that satan is *really* going to regret it?) In general, the choice of how much authority we walk in is now ours- how deeply are we going to walk in agreement with Jesus' heart and his wisdom?

However, most believers allow the enemy to have a lot of legal leeway in the name of self-indulgence, sinful false comforts, and entitlements. The first common way the enemy is able to shut down living faith in believers is through our refusal to forgive, bitterness, and offense. Jesus warned that we MUST forgive in order to stay free. The alternative is to give in to a root of bitterness and offense that eventually will poison all of our relationships including our relationship with Jesus. The one who refused to forgive was given over to the tormentors in Matthew 18.

The second common way the enemy is able to usurp authority from believers is through habitual sin and compromise. For example, the Bible tells us that any type of sexual activity outside of marriage is sin (sexual immorality). Yet this generation faces a flood-tide of internet pornography and other sexual sin capable of doing tremendous damage to the soul very quickly. One of the ways we can love Jesus is by honoring him by what we do with our bodies.

The third most common way the enemy usurps authority is by using extremely negative events in our lives when we are vulnerable to create a stronghold of lies. Since we live on planet earth, negative things happen as the result of our hostile environment and other peoples' sinful choices. For example, in my own life, I had to deal with an extremely powerful stronghold of rejection that was rooted in abandonment from South Korea. Thus a deeply rooted false belief system leading to an expectation of rejection over the years was able to grow.

The forth most common way the enemy usurps authority is through curses and familiar spirits passed down generational family lines. Certain sins such as idolatry, sorcery, and anti-Semitism produce iniquity (weakness or vulnerability) that is passed down from generation to generation that the enemy takes advantage of.

Jesus made some radical and rather offensive statements related to forsaking family (if necessary) for the sake of the Gospel. These curses and any generational sin patterns can be broken by identifying with the finished work of Jesus.

We don't need to put up with satan continuing his "rebel" tactics of stealing, killing, and destroying things in our lives. Usually it simply means repenting of sin (including that of unbelief or bitterness), exposing and renouncing the deception of satan, and telling him to leave. However, we must make lifestyle changes so that the enemy does not come back in. For example, if we had a habit of sexual immorality and we got set free, we need to discard or guard any things that cause us to be tempted in that area. (For example, we put internet software on our computer that blocks pornography and find someone to hold us accountable.)

Exercising our spiritual authority on earth:

When God put Adam and Eve in the garden of Eden, his first command was that they would take dominion of the earth and subdue it. God made people with a desire to cultivate and develop the material, natural resources of the earth. God also gave humanity general delegated authority over what happens on the earth:

The highest heavens belong to the LORD, but the earth he has given to mankind. (Psalm 115:16)

God is just even to the unjust- God rules in the highest heavens and releases heavenly decrees. However, they will not be executed on the earth unless God finds someone to agree with Him on the earth. Jesus will not come back to rule the earth until His natural-born brothers invite Him to come back and every other scripture is fulfilled.

The potential scope of our authority on behalf of the true King on the earth is beyond our wildest imagination. God uses His power (that backs up His authority) to protect us, to build us up, to bless us, and remove all that hinders love. In the gospels, we find Jesus as a man modeling what it means to operate in the authority, backed up by the power of the Holy Spirit.

Authority over sickness and disease

A quick read through of the synoptic Gospels shows a trail of people who experienced physical healing. One of the first ways God revealed His name to Israel was The LORD our Healer. Blind eyes opened, deaf ears were opened. The lame walked. Every disease including leprosy was healed. Jesus would go into places and everyone was healed. Jesus would go into other places and because of unbelief, not much happened.

In the same way, His servants today operate can walk in the same authority. People such as Reinhard Bonnke and Heidi Bakker regularly see serious healing of all types of diseases using the name of Jesus. Beginning in 2012, I have been in the company of about 10 personal friends who frequently see people experience the healing power of God in the context of evangelism. In one case, several of us prayed for a man named "Glen" who was diagnosed with terminal (Stage IV) bone cancer by a doctor.

The day after the prayer, Glen went back to the doctor and the terminal bone cancer diagnosis was replaced with a new diagnosis of "shocked doctor syndrome". In the previous month, the blood tests showed that his cancer cell count was 267 cpm. Now the tests showed a cancer cell count of 0. God had physically healed him and gave him new bone marrow.

Authority over demons:

Related to authority over sickness is exercising authority over the demonic realm. Many of Jesus' healings involved casting out demons. Jesus found a man out of his mind and the demon named "Legion" manifested. Jesus cast the demon out and the people found the man in his right mind and they were very afraid. The Apostle Paul confronted the demonized culture of Ephesus in Acts 19. Many extraordinary miracles occurred in the city and demons were cast out- impacting the whole economic climate of the city and causing a riot.

God still gives people authority over demons through the name of Jesus. In Argentina, Carlos Annacondia openly challenged demons in open-air evangelism campaigns in the 1990's. Carlos would confront the powers behind witchcraft in a city and hundreds of people would fall to the ground and begin manifesting. In my own ministry, its rather amazing to see how many people I've seen healed in prayer lines and healing rooms when people renounce bitterness, or association with witchcraft. After the spirit is cast out, they are instantly healed. I simply speak the name of Jesus in obedience and the demons flee.

Authority over the natural realm

While on earth, Jesus exercised authority over the physical environment as well. Two of the more notable miracles include Jesus calming the seas (by walking on them) and Jesus multiplying the five loaves and two fishes to feed 5,000 men. In Acts 28, Paul was bitten by a deadly snake, but the poison did not affect him.

There are a number of occasions in the Old Testament where God stepped in and altered what naturally occurs.

In modern days, God still exercises power and authority over the physical environment through his servants at the name of Jesus. A 2012 ministry trip to Florida led by Rodney nearly got cancelled due to money issues, but Rodney courageously continued the outreach anyway. On this outreach, Jesus put me and other intercessors "on alert" related to the weather patterns on a Friday evening. A huge storm came towards the outdoor outreach site with heavy rain, wind, and lightning. Looking like an idiot, I stood up and prayed against the storm in the name of Jesus and the clouds responded with violent motion all around. The local pastor overseeing the outreach later investigated and found that it had rained in every direction except where we were preaching the gospel. Many people gave their lives to Jesus that weekend and bodies were healed.

Authority over death

Jesus exercised authority over death as He went to the cross, died, and was raised from the dead in the power of the Holy Spirit with a resurrection body. Of course, Jesus raised a few people from the dead (Jarius's daughter, Lazarus) as signs that death is not the final authority in the human existence. Peter and Paul also raised people from the dead under the authority of the name of Jesus.

In our day, David Hogan's ministry in Mexico has raised several hundred people from the dead at the mighty name of Jesus. A powerful intercessor named Pam (now with Jesus) raised several premature babies from the dead in Minneapolis. In another case an older couple in the IHOP-KC community, were at Burger King when a guy stopped breathing and his heart stopped beating. Others could not revive him. This couple then rebuked the spirit of death and breath came back into the man. As we approach the end of the age, I believe that many will operate in the anointing to "ruin funerals" at the name of Jesus.

At the name of Jesus, EVERY knee will bow. We have that privilege of submitting to his gracious authority now and using His delegated authority to do His will. Yet most of us do not consistently walk in this type of spiritual authority, but only on special occasions.

Expanding the exercise of our spiritual authority: Going deeper in agreement with Jesus

Jesus Christ has set us free and given us personal authority over our lives. However, if we want to be entrusted with more, we must be faithful to follow through in obedience to Jesus. By bringing things directly under our control into submission to the leadership of Jesus, we will gain more freedom to exercise His authority over life situations. Why should Jesus take our obedience to "heal the sick" seriously if we aren't bringing other areas of our lives into obedience to Jesus? God wants to entrust more authority to every member of the body of Christ. Here are ways we can gain or expand the exercise of our spiritual authority in Jesus to bless others:

Practice persevering, faithful obedience. Paul said that anyone who has been given a trust from Jesus must prove faithful. Jesus said if we are faithful in little, we will be faithful with much. Jesus also told the parable of the unjust judge in Luke 18 related to faithfulness at his return. God deliberately sets up unfair and difficult circumstances- often using satan and his demons unwittingly (who think its an opportunity to get revenge by really hurting us) to do this. God does this to test our faithfulness to Him for the sake of promotion.

Grow in Wisdom/experience: The scripture says that Jesus as a young man, grew in favor with God and with man. Closely related to perseverance and faithfulness is growth in wisdom and experience. However without the Spirit of Wisdom, many of our experiences are simply in the category of "what not" to do. Faithfulness combined with the Spirit of Wisdom (through success and failures) gives us a living history to instruct others with.

Grow in the depth of obedience: Someone who fasted and prayed in agreement with Jesus will have more authority in a spiritual battle than someone who only prayed. For example, in a recent evangelism program, a young man named Joshua saw a cancerous tumor disappear and saw a large number of people give their lives to Jesus-far more than anyone else in the program. I also learned that this young man had done a few fasts in excess of 21 days to agree with Jesus in his first year of serving Jesus after being lost. This young man's depth of obedience in his first year of following Jesus was greater than anything I did in my first year of following Jesus.

Submit to those in authority over us: Scripture says that all authority is from God (Romans 13:1)- including authorities that we disagree with. God gives groups of people (from 5 to 500,000,000) the leadership that they deserve- as either a blessing or a curse. Learning how to submit to authority that we do not agree with requires wisdom and humility. Learning how to submit to leadership who is at war with Jesus and us requires great wisdom and humility- like David (with Saul) or Daniel (with Nebuchadnezzar). Jesus submitted to the Father's authority to the utter-most and exercises the great authority as well.

Overcome difficulty and trials. Jesus repeatedly gave the promise of great eternal rewards to those who overcome in Revelation 2 and 3 which include a great measure of authority over nations. Paul wrote about comforting others with the comfort we have received (1 Corinthians 1:3-6). When we overcome something, we gain authority to help others more easily gain victory as well. Paul boasted about his basis for authority in 2 Corinthians 11- how had experienced and overcome pain and hardship by the power of the Holy Spirit.

Understand the limits of our authority: God gives all of us authority to heal the sick, cast out demons, prophesy, and do other things to make Jesus known in word and deed. However it does not mean we have authority to go beyond what the scriptures say we have. Many people have presumptuously gone beyond the boundaries of their authority granted by Jesus and had experiences much like the Jewish exorcists in Acts 19:13-16.

Using the name of Jesus, we have access to the unlimited power of the Holy Spirit to do all of God's will, God's way. Exercising God's delegated authority in partnership with Him was meant to fill our hearts with joy. The disciples came back to Jesus rejoicing in Luke 10 after seeing God back up their words with power. That God entrusts such authority to beloved ones who are still growing in humility and maturity is a statement of how valuable you truly are to God of the heavens and the earth.

8

EXPOSING WITCHCRAFT

The woman in the dirty white bridal dress was furious. She went up to the sheriff's deputy pointing at the guy dressed in a maroon pullover: "Arrest him! Arrest him! He's ruining everything!"

"You may not like him, but I can't do anything to him because he is simply standing on the property. He's not breaking the law."

She continued to yell and throw a tirade as effective evangelism continued throughout the night in the West Bottoms of Kansas City.

This was in contrast to the first hour of evangelistic outreach. The owners who put on the annual KC "Haunted House" extravaganza had blocked off the streets as "private property" to prevent evangelism with trespassing laws on public roads. For "some reason", the haunted house staff was able to pick out those who were there to share the Gospel of Jesus Christ. A number of our team were escorted off the property and threatened with arrest by the police officers. Hearts were hard and people resistant to hearing God's good news.

Recognizing that the haunted house staff were actually doing sorcery (casting spells and interacting with demons) to help them, I stopped evangelizing and began praying in tongues, binding the demonic spirits from functioning. Suddenly, the staff was no longer able to cast spells or effectively do divination. Hearts were now suddenly receptive to the Gospel. During that last hour, over a dozen people gave their lives to Jesus on Halloween weekend, right at "the Edge of Hell".

A pandemic of witchcraft and sorcery in society:

We get the word "Pharmacy" from a Greek word for "sorcery" or hidden knowledge. Modern medicine through scientific discovery is a gift from God- and God undoubtedly saved many lives through modern medicine. However, with prescription medication has come an explosion of illegal drugs along with the abuse of legal ones. Satan has taken advantage of this explosion of illicit drugs to put millions in the bondage of looking for the next "emotional high". Many of these substances open up the user's lives to interaction with demons.

Over the last few decades, there has been a spiritual revival in America, but it has not been a Christian one. In the 1980's and early 1990's when I grew up, sorcery and witchcraft were relegated to a "nerd" fringe that played spooky games such as *Dungeons and Dragons*. Cartoons such as *Master's of the Universe, Voltron,* and *Smurfs* exposed a generation to magick, but the true occultic nature of such shows was veiled. With the exception of an occasional horoscope in the local newspaper, the occult was rather hidden.

However, over the last few decades, sorcery and witchcraft has come out of the closet. J.K. Rowling introduced a whole generation to the world of the occult and witchcraft through her *Harry Potter* series. *World of Warcraft* is an online game involving the occult realm which has millions of subscribers. Psychic hotlines and fortune-telling that were once relegated to late night television is now mainstream business of America. Primetime TV in America now features shows with occult overtones.

Fueling the explosion of witchcraft in America is the shedding of innocent blood through abortion. Abortion was viewed as a back-alley event before the U.S. government legalized it in 1973 through *Roe vs. Wade.* Since then over 50 million babies have been legally murdered in the United States. Scripture is clear that the shedding of innocent blood fuels demonic activity and brings a curse upon the land (see Num.35:33; Deut. 19:10; Ps 106:36-40; 2 Kings 24:3-4). It is no accident that it was in 1973 *The Exorcist* came out and became one of the highest-grossing horror movies of all times-beginning the exposure of a whole generation to satanism and sorcery.

Scripture is clear that interaction with demons through divination or occult practices is forbidden and brings a curse (Deut. 13:1-5, 18:10-12; Lev. 19:1, 20:6.). The apostle Paul gave instructions to the Corinthians to avoid feasts in celebration of false gods in the name of "Christian freedom" because of its association with sorcery and idolatry that provokes God's jealous anger for our lives (1 Cor.10:14-22).

In a society where knowledge is exploding and global competition is increasing, everyone is looking to gain "an edge" over the competition. Hence, many have turned to the supernatural for guidance. A post-modern generation knows that there is "something" out there beyond the physical, material world. Yet, this same post-modern generation has found very little authentic spirituality within much of the Church of Jesus Christ. Instead, most simply find a bunch of religious rules, rituals, and traditions; a form of godliness that is devoid of power. In looking elsewhere, a whole generation is being swept into more direct involvement with demonic oppression.

The Church in the West has protested, but has been generally powerless to stop this floodtide of evil. Why? The first problem is that much of the Body of Christ in the West believes in the false doctrine of Cessationism- the belief that the signs and wonders of the Bible ceased with the apostles once the scriptures were written. There are whole denominations who falsely belief that any modern-day manifestations of supernatural power and authority are automatically "of the devil". Without the supernatural presence and power of God, what is left is humanism dressed up in religious tradition. Many of these denominations are being swept away into compromising other parts of the teaching of scripture.

The Body of Christ is not automatically immune:

Of course there are an increasing number in the Church from the "western world" that believe in the supernatural power of God. However there is a second problem that is far more subtle: Much of the Body of Christ in the West is vulnerable to the counter-attack of satan through sorcery and witchcraft.

To illustrate, on January 27th, 2008 IHOP-KC closed on the acquisition of the "Truman property" a miraculous sign and wonder related to God's end-time purposes for the Jewish people. Harry S. Truman was the U.S. president and "political intercessor" responsible for Israel being re-established as a nation with a homeland in the Middle East. On January 27th, 1958 Harry S. Truman sold the 125 acre piece of property to a Jewish family. Fifty years later to the day, IHOP-KC acquired the property debt free as a sign of jubilee.

A few days later, a huge outbreak of sickness struck the IHOP-KC mission base. A large percentage of the whole base experienced significant illness- whole worship teams were being taken out by sickness-for up to a week. Roughly a dozen people ended up hospitalized and at least one person ended up dying from sicknesses acquired during this period.

Special prayer meetings were initiated to stop the attack of sickness and disease. We used our authority in Christ and the sickness outbreak stopped. In the wake of this incident, some hard questions need to be asked: *Why did this happen? Is God trying to say anything important in this? Is there anyway to protect the community from this sort of spiritual attack from happening again?*

Circumstantially, God had openly displayed his power related to the elections of South Korea. Mike Bickle had just finished *Call to All Orlando* where top missions leaders recognized how important continuous worship and prayer was to finishing the great commission. Mike was becoming known around the world as a global prayer ministry leader which also involved tremendous change. With large amounts of change and opportunity came the associated typical human relational dynamics.

Meanwhile, Harry S. Truman was a noble U.S. President who took many unpopular but righteous stands. Asking for the grace of God to help him, he stood against global opinion and Israel was re-established as a sovereign nation in 1948.

However, historical records are clear that Harry S. Truman was a 33rd degree Freemason. He considered being named as the main leader over the Grand Lodge in Missouri to be an incredibly huge honor. In the 1940's, freemasonry simply looked like another fraternity of political and business associations with "goofy rituals".

The problem is that since then, we have learned that freemasonry is associated with idolatry, witchcraft, greed, and lust for power. At the top levels, freemasonry is about direct service to satan. Whole pieces of land have been dedicated and cities such as Washington DC are laid out in honor of freemasonry. Idolatry and sorcery brings a curse that includes health problems. Many authors have written books exposing freemasonry and many have received healing and deliverance when they renounced it.

Circumstantially, the enemy was really upset at IHOP-KC as major breakthrough had just occurred. We were in new "unknown" territory spiritually. Circumstantially with all of the changes and the associated human dynamics, we were vulnerable to a destructive counter-attack of satan through high-level witchcraft. It's no surprise that the enemy took advantage of the opportunity presented.

Witchcraft as a work of the flesh: rebellion against authority, misused authority, and usurped authority

To gain insight into why the Body of Christ can still be vulnerable to witchcraft especially in the midst of transition, we need to look at the scriptures. Galatians 5:19-21 includes witchcraft as a "work of the flesh" with other types of sin- it is part of human sinful nature to reject, misuse, or usurp authority.

When the Bible was written, the cultures of the near-east were steeped in sorcery, divination, and idolatry. God thundered from Heaven on Mt. Sinai:

"You shall not misuse the name of the LORD your God, for the LORD will not hold anyone guiltless who misuses his name. (Exodus 20:7)

While contemporary church culture uses this commandment against foul language and cursing, there is a much deeper issue at stake here: the misuse of delegated authority, rebellion, and usurped authority. This is a commandment to avoid sin related to authority.

In the Old Testament, if there was a dispute, that was unsolvable, they could bring parties together and have them take an oath in the name of the LORD to tell the whole truth before the priests and judges. The oath implied if they were deceptive in any way, that God could then bring judgment against them. Jesus called us to a level of truthfulness and integrity in Matthew 5:33-36 so that our word would be just as good as an oath in relating to others. (Jesus did not forbid the taking of civil oaths.) Jesus then rebuked the religious leaders for their hypocrisy in misusing oaths for selfish gain (and so dishonoring the God of Israel) in Matthew 23:16-22.

In 1 Samuel 15, God commanded (and gave grace for) Saul to completely take out the Amalekites because of their idolatry, witchcraft, and unrepentant wickedness. Of course, we find that Saul did not take care of business, but used God's delegated authority for selfish gain at the expense of Israel's future. King Agag was kept alive and his descendents (who were in deep agreement with wickedness) were not wiped out. One of his descendents, named Haman, plotted to wipe out Israel in the book of Esther.

Of course, the LORD was very angry and talked to His prophet Samuel about it. Samuel later confronted Saul who claimed that he had obeyed the Lord fully. Samuel replied:

Does the LORD delight in burnt offerings and sacrifices, as much as in obeying the voice of the LORD?
To obey is better than sacrifice, and to heed is better than the fat of rams.
23 For rebellion is like the sin of divination, and arrogance like the evil of idolatry.
Because you have rejected the word of the LORD, he has rejected you as king."(1 Samuel 15:22-23)

Going forward in time, we find Saul in the witch's house at the end of the book. He had completely rejected God's counsel and was now trying to directly interact with demonic powers.

The most direct application of this passage is related to rebellion- it is like witchcraft. We all probably experienced negative consequences of rebellion growing up. We would do something as

83

a child that mom and dad told us not to do, and our parents would then follow through with something that caused us to cry in sadness. Some of us experienced "the board of education on the seat of learning". Others of us got grounded (and are STILL grounded).

Many of us have experienced bad consequences related to rebellion. Yet in many Charismatic/Pentecostal streams, people can cheaply justify rebellion to delegated authority (who asks them to do something they don't like) by claiming "God told me". This is a clear example of misusing the name of the LORD to manipulate. Often the fruit of these actions is division and great wounding of relationships. In the midst of a situation like this, the enemy has an easy temporal victory.

Even if God promised something, it doesn't mean I need to make a prophetic promise happen through setting things up my way. In my experience, God actually enjoys it when we "test God's promises" by submitting to godly human delegated authority and deliberately making it "harder" for God to fulfill them in the natural. Unless their instructions contradict the clear teaching of scripture, we should trust God's leadership through our delegated leaders.

A second application of this passage related to witchcraft is the misuse of authority. Jesus was full of compassion for people who were broken as he walked on the earth. However, he had stinging rebukes for the leadership of Israel who were misusing their authority for selfish gain at the expense of the people. Jesus warned:

But if anyone causes one of these little ones who believe in me to sin, it would be better for him to have a large millstone hung around his neck and to be drowned in the depths of the sea. (Matthew 18:6)

Clearly, leaders who misuse authority to manipulate other people under their leadership into sin is a very serious issue to Him. Jesus later warned his apostolic leadership team:

But suppose that servant (apostolic leader) is wicked and says to himself, 'My master is staying away a long time', and he begins to beat his fellow servants and to eat and drink with the drunkards. The master of that servant will come on a day when he does not expect him and at an hour he is not aware of. He will cut him to pieces and assign him a place with the hypocrites, where there will be weeping and gnashing of teeth. (Matthew 24:48-51)

Direct authority over people from Jesus is a great privilege, but also a very serious responsibility with heightened accountability.

A third application of how authority is misused or usurped is through deception, manipulation, and intimidation. First found in Genesis 3, satan usurped authority from Adam and Eve by manipulating what God said. Ever since the first sibling rivalry between Cain and Abel, people have always been trying to "one up" and usurp each other. Even the disciples were not immune to this in the midst of their "discussions" on who would be the greatest. We need to look at the character of Jacob to understand this:

In Genesis 25, we find Jacob and Esau wrestling in Rebekah's womb. Surely this uncomfortable feeling caused Rebekah to ask God, "What's going on?" The LORD replied,

"Two nations are in your womb, and two peoples from within you will be separated; one people will be stronger than the other, and the older will serve the younger." (Genesis 25:23)

When Jacob and Esau came out of the womb, they were fighting for the birthright. Esau came out first and then Jacob. However, Esau then sold his birthright for a pot of stew. Esau then married a Hittite woman that was a source of grief to Isaac and Rebekah (Genesis 26:34-35).

We learn later that Isaac thought that he was about to die and wanted to bless his older son Esau. Meanwhile Rebekah overheard this. Rebekah and Jacob then schemed to get Isaac to bless Jacob instead of Esau before he died-presuming he was about to die quickly. Jacob did get Isaac's blessing of the first-born and Esau a prophecy.

God's later commentary is that he loved Jacob but hated Esau (Mal 1:1-5; Heb.12:16-17). Why? Esau cared nothing about the anointing and promises of God. Jacob cared deeply and desperately wanted them-even willing to manipulate others to get them. What Jacob did not realize was that God was faithful and true and that God hates falsehood. Thus God sent Jacob on a 21 year journey to experience what it is like to serve under a man (Laban) who was very manipulative and thus oppressive. It was only after Jacob wrestled with God and his manipulative nature was confronted could he receive the prophetic birthright.

A warning to Mike Bickle in 1990:

God gave Mike Bickle a prophetic warning that he recorded in the notes of prophetic history session 3 of IHOP-KC's 10 year anniversary celebration:

*At 4 AM on October 5, 1990, the Lord appeared to me in a trance. Suddenly the Lord was standing before me, looking straight into my eyes and said, **"No one with a control spirit can fully experience My kingdom."** He paused 3 seconds, the words "possessiveness and religious opinions" came clearly to me.*

*Next, the Lord said, **"All personal rights must be relinquished."** The verse came instantly to me, "They will cast their crowns before My throne" (Rev. 4:10). The Lord then said, **"I have a controversy with My people."** The Spirit said, "The earth is the Lord's, and all it contains. (Ps. 24:1). Only Jesus owns the ministries, the buildings, the money, the people and the future".*

When the trance lifted, then the power of God rushed through me, violently shaking my entire body for about 15 seconds. I reached with my left hand to stop the shaking in my right hand! The Spirit said, "I am going to give power demonstrations to back up this truth."[2]

All this happened while Mike Bickle was on a major ministry trip with John Wimber in Great Britain. Mike gave this word multiple times and gave ministry time for leaders who had difficulty with control. With their cover blown, demons manifested in response to the anointing of the Spirit. Bob Jones (later) told Mike,

"The Lord took you up Jacob's ladder and told you He will release power to deal with Jacob spirit. He said there is a swindler spirit that is going to be dealt with in power."[3]

This encounter was a stern warning against the misuse of spiritual power or authority to manipulate other people for selfish gain. Anyone using spiritual power or authority (including incidents where God released power by the Holy Spirit) for the sake of manipulating others to do our will is suddenly in agreement with the "wisdom of satan". Thus they are now a vulnerable target to getting hit by curses through witches, warlocks, shamans, and other servants of satan practicing sorcery.

God is not withholding anything good from His Bride. The problem is within us. One of the primary reasons why God has not released widespread, awesome demonstrations of power in response to delegated authority is because of mercy for us. God is faithful to protect His servants from conceit and getting destroyed

---

[2] Used by permission; http://mikebickle.org/faq/
[3] ibid.

by unperceived counter-attacks of servants of satan. Of course, this also means that if we can overcome these obstacles by the grace of God, incredibly great things will happen!

⑨

OVERCOMING WITCHCRAFT

In the last few chapters we have learned that Jesus has far superior power and authority to satan. While we do not have physical power over satan, God has given us access to using this unlimited spiritual authority in Jesus Christ to do His will because we are his beloved ones. However, the level of manifested authority (and the power of the Holy Spirit) varies greatly from one believer to another based on the depth and consistency of our obedience. With great manifest authority comes great responsibility.

Satan uses his trickery to get us to sin related to operating with authority. As the Body of Christ, we do not have automatic immunity to satan's attack through witchcraft. Rebellion, the misuse of authority to oppress others, and usurping authority through intimidation and manipulation leave us open to the attack of satan through sorcery. However, we are not defenseless against the attacks of sorcery from the enemy.

The supremacy of Jesus over sorcery and witchcraft

We do not need to be afraid of the tricks of the enemy. One of his tricks for those who have been hit by the enemy is fear and deception. The enemy will attempt to lie- that he is much more powerful than Jesus. The book of Acts tells a number of stories about how ministers of the gospel went head-to head in direct spiritual warfare with mediums and sorcerers.

Moving to our day, I've already told the story from the *Edge of Hell* in 2011. I want to tell a few more stories that illustrate the supremacy of Jesus Christ over every form of witchcraft and sorcery:

Santi-Cali-Gon Days 2010

Every year, the city of Independence Missouri hosts a huge celebration over Labor Day weekend called Santa-Cali-Gon Days.

Tens of thousands of people go to the city streets to have one last party before fall starts. The festival has a carnival and many food vendors, and other booths selling things or promoting causes.

That year, we had a booth for the IHOP-KC with the evangelism department and involving the school of ministry. We were offering free prayer and prophecy. I noticed that we were located next to the psychic booth- a woman and her assistants were there to do fortune telling and charging money. Our spirits were troubled- what should we do now?

In the midst of set up, God prophetically gave me the name of the main woman we'll call "Sarah" (name has been changed) practicing divination next to our booth. The Holy Spirit also gave me some details related to her background and so I could go attempt to minister to her. I went over to her booth. Sarah came over to me and asked with a smirk, "Do you want me to tell your fortune?"

I replied, "No, but God wants you to know…." I then proceeded to download what God was telling me about Sarah. Immediately, bitterness and pain rose up inside of her and she instantly "shut down" and did not want to talk to me. It was as if the demonic spirit communicating with her warned that I was a threat.

Later that weekend, YWAM did a stage presentation of the gospel right next to the psychic booth and dozens of people came to the Lord. Sarah ended up complaining to the city that her "business" of divination was ruined from our evangelism booth that year.

Confrontation with freemasonry at IHOP-KC in 2013

As part of my own service at IHOP-KC, I serve on the Korean prophecy teams where we invite guests to come and receive prophetic ministry. Over Super Bowl weekend, I was serving with a young woman who did not have a lot of experience in prophecy. Into the prophecy room came "Sam" (name has been changed) with long facial hair, weird clothing, a huge ring on his middle finger, and a huge smirk. Next to him was a younger, smaller guy named "Tim" (name has been changed) who looked a bit dazed and confused. A closer look at the man's ring revealed that it had the classic freemasonry symbol. With him came a massive spiritual presence that was clearly not the "Holy Spirit".

How was I supposed to be "encouraging, comforting, or edifying" in the face of someone who was in blatant agreement with demonic forces? I asked him what it was. After he "played dumb", I exhorted him to turn from idolatry related to freemasonry and to the One True God. My rattled partner did the same thing.

Meanwhile, Tim was suddenly not "hoodwinked" by this guy anymore and asked him to leave. Sam refused and said in a deep guttural voice, "No". I then rose up and "invited him to leave" (where I was going to call security if he did not). He eventually left and we ministered to Tim who could now see the malevolent plot against him through "Sam".

It was clear that "Sam" was on assignment from the enemy. The next day, worship leader Misty Edwards called this guy out from the platform and invited him to repent. He tried to make a relational bond with me (by trying to give me a hug) but that simply did not work as I broke his soulish move off. A day later, I found "Sam" trying to seduce one of my friends and I took the young guy aside to explain what was going on.

Finally, that Monday, I informed some of the leadership of IHOP-KC and we prayed to bind the spirits and forbidding him to come back to try to seduce people. That evening, my friend Josh and other leaders in the prayer room caught this man continuing his witchcraft and after he refused to stop he was escorted off the property by the security team.

New Orleans 2013

In New Orleans, we stayed at the NOLA House of Prayer and did evangelism during Mardi Gras. God had raised up a friend who bought us free plane tickets to go to New Orleans. God used the team mightily to release salvation, healing, and deliverance to many who had come for Mardi Gras. God released a number of significant miracles as one guy with a cane staggered onto the ferry to get across the river. Our team prayed and he was totally healed on the ferry ride. He walked off, celebrating and carrying his cane. Another guy with metal rods in his legs (and in great pain) could suddenly move his body normally without pain after receiving prayer at the name of Jesus.

Of course this stirred up the enemy and those who ignorantly obey him. One guy tried to put a curse on our group on the street. We turned and looked at him and the guy went running. In another case, team members went head-to head spiritually with a fortune-teller. The fortune teller (accustomed to being right through a spirit of divination) was wrong while we prophetically called him out and planted a deep seed of the gospel. Again, dozens of people were swept into the Kingdom in the midst of an environment filled with lawlessness, rebellion, and sorcery.

From these stories, and many others, we can be certain that God's power is far superior to the power of satan. God's weakest servants have far more power and authority available to them than even satan's "top spiritual generals" on the earth. The problem is that so often we are in subtle compromise with deception to manipulate or intimidate. Voluntarily, we end up in agreement (and giving over authority) to satan.

Is manipulation and intimidation inevitable?

The other day, I was watching an old Isuzu commercial involving a lie detector machine on *you tube.* After describing the awesome facts of the truck he is trying to tell, Joe Isuzu finishes the commercial with, "See, you can trust me." Of course, the lie detector machine goes off and gives Joe the shock of his life.

In 2008, there was a game show, *The Moment of Truth.* On the surface, the game show seems simple: contestants took a polygraph test before coming on the show. During the polygraph test, they ask around 50 questions of increasing invasiveness and sensitivity. Then 21 (or 22) questions are selected from the polygraph examination. The result is that people are confronted with emotionally difficult and embarrassing questions live before all of America and family members.

All a contestant has to do is answer 21 questions truthfully with a "yes" or "no" (to the best of their understanding) and they will win $500,000. The first set of 6 questions is worth $10,000, the second set of 5, $25,000, the third set of 4, $100,000, the forth set of 3 questions $200,000 the fifth set of 2 questions $350,000, and the final question $500,000. A contestant could stop at any time after the first 6 questions and take the money. However, if the contestant was lying according to the lie-detector test, the game was immediately over and the contestant lost the money they had earned from telling previous truthful answers.

As the levels progress and the money increases, the contestant is faced with a key question: Do I want to face another painful and embarrassing question (that could ruin how other people perceive me, future opportunities etc.) or would I rather take the money earned from answering previous (difficult, painful, and embarrassing) questions truthfully? I watched part of the show as someone with a gambling issue told the bitter truth about it before all of America (and got the most money of any contestant on the show). These shows lend credence to the motto, "the truth hurts".

Underlying the question is another deeper question, *how much does the Body of Christ love truth, no matter how much it hurts?* To avoid painful and embarrassing truth issues we often cover it up with subtle manipulation and intimidation. Yet it is compromise with deception, manipulation, and intimidation that makes us vulnerable to attacks of the occult and witchcraft. Why? I believe scripture tells us two key issues:

1. The fear of man

If you are like me, I definitely prefer to be "liked" than in the middle of a controversy and conflict. In many cultures, there is a strong cultural value of "polite-ness" and political correct-ness. In shame-based cultures, "saving face" is a big issue. It is considered culturally acceptable to "fudge the truth" so that you end up looking better.

Since we all like the emotional euphoria of "being liked" (more on this issue of relational bonding in the next chapter), we then strive to consistently experience this emotion. The problem is that relationships tend to be messy and the truth is often embarrassing. The "good feeling" soul-ties provide cover and excuses on why we should cover things up-and we have the early stages of building a stronghold of intimidation and manipulation. Scripture warns:

Fear of man will prove to be a snare, but whoever trusts in the LORD is kept safe. (Proverbs 29:25)

Even as we get more successful, the stakes get higher with initiatives, boundaries, and allocation of resources at stake. Do we fear what people will do/give us or do we deeply fear the LORD? The scripture above leads us to a second key reason why we usually give in to subtle manipulation or intimidation.

2. Unbelief

For true disciples of Jesus, most of us do not doubt that He is real and that the Bible is true- we've experienced the truth of the Bible. The issue of belief or unbelief is much more subtle related to manipulation/ intimidation of others: *We don't believe that God's leadership involves the intimate, important details in our lives.*

We theoretically believe that God supernaturally provides all the resources, wealth, and materials for all of us to do His will and fulfill the dreams of our lives. Yet when it comes to real life issues involving the physical, material realm we don't believe He really cares. Since dramatic interventions of God are rare (and usually overwhelming), we conclude in the now that it is more important to manipulate/intimidate to get things done.

Unbelief is behind rebellion. *Why should I submit to this authority that I disagree with (and is even quite oppressive)?* We forget that God specifically knows this leader and formed their emotional make up and personality traits. God also knows about their weaknesses and personality "quirks". Behind the bitterness of rebellion is a false belief system that does not believe that God can lead my life perfectly using the leader who has "issues".

Unbelief is behind the misuse of spiritual authority for selfish gain in oppressing others. In extreme cases, it can lead to mass murder and destruction. Hitler was offered a legacy that would last over 1,000 years from satan- not really believing that God has a specific plan for the Jewish people. Kim-Jung II believed he was a god and the eternal president of North Korea. In partnership with demons and the cultural norms, he deceived a people group and a whole nation has suffered greatly for this over the last few decades.

The sea of glass and Jacob's wrestling match: a key to victory

So how do we gain victory over the fear of man and associated unbelief? An obscure concept may hold the key- John saw a sea of glass.

Also before the throne, there was what looked like a sea of glass, clear as crystal. (Rev. 4:6)

I saw something like a sea of glass mingled with fire and, standing beside the sea, those who had been victorious over the beast.... (Rev. 15:2)

God revealed dimensions of the Sea to the three critical generations (the generations of Moses, Ezekiel, and the apostles) in the midst of coming great trouble and chaos. I believe this generation will understand and experience much more related to the sea of glass than the previous ones.

We need to look at the crystal sea from natural eyes to get understanding of the sea of glass. On a completely calm day (no wind), a body of water can look like a sheet of glass. The water can function as a perfect mirror. At some of our national memorials and monuments we have reflecting pools- still water that functions as a mirror.

God showed his prophets the sea of glass as a message of complete calm and peace in the heart of God in the midst of his fiery emotions towards us and radiant wisdom to bring forth righteousness. There is no doubt in the heart of God (reflected in the calm crystal sea) that He will accomplish His eternal purposes. It is effortless for God to crush His adversaries. God has all the power, wisdom, knowledge, riches, and time to fulfill His eternal purposes precisely without violating anyone's free will.

However, the sea of glass also speaks of the transparency of those standing on it. God knows everything about us that we know- and many things about us that we do not know. When Adam sinned in Genesis 3, the first thing that he lost was that pure, innocent transparent communion with God. Ashamed at what instantly happened, they hid from God. Jesus went to the cross to restore that unbroken communion.

The idea of God knowing the flaws and brokenness in our lives is frightening. The idea of either God or other people knowing the stuff in our lives and then making decisions that affect us is completely horrifying. How many have heard the sports cliché of how our team won the championship by exploiting the other teams' weaknesses? This is how the world system typically works- and we often assume that God is like this.

Last chapter, I mentioned that God sent Jacob on a 21 year journey to deal with his deceiving nature at the hands of another oppressive deceiver named Laban. Things came to a head where Jacob out-deceived the deceiver Laban and was once again running for his life with his family. Then there was the issue of Esau who wanted to kill him. The night before he met Esau again, Jacob got into a wrestling match with a "mystery man" physically, emotionally, and spiritually. He still could not live without the blessing of God.

In the midst of the wrestling, the "mystery man" touched Jacob's hip and it was wrenched out of its socket and demanded that he let go of him. By now, Jacob knew this was no ordinary "man" he was wrestling with. He would rather die than live without the blessing. However this mystery man asked him a question perhaps more agonizing than death: *What is your name?*

Within a name is identity, his nature. At that terrible moment, Jacob understood deeply what his nature was like. Jacob knew that he was a manipulator and deceiver. Jacob also finally understood that the one he wanted a blessing from hated manipulation and deception. Finally, Jacob realized there was no way that he could manipulate this man into blessing him.

What Jacob discovered next was that at the core of the Kingdom of Heaven is: God knows all about us and yet deeply desires us with tender affection. In Psalm 132, God is called "The Mighty One of Jacob"- unashamed of our brokenness and weakness. This same God is wisely leading us unto his fullness forever. On the sea of glass, we will finally know God and each other as we are fully known by God. Revelation 7 depicts the result of people who fully understand this:

After this, I looked and there before me was a great multitude that no one could count, from every nation, tribe, people and language standing before the throne and in front of the Lamb. They were wearing white robes and were holding palm branches in their hands. And they cried on in a loud voice:

"Salvation belongs to our God, who sits on the throne, and to the Lamb."(Revelation 7:9-10)

At the very end, a people are completely transparent before God and each other. The truth is fully known and yet there we are standing on the sea of glass, unashamed before God and each other, faces beaming with joy and peace.

Who says we can't live in this reality *in this age* before God and people? Jesus came walking on the earth, full of grace and truth. Groups of people can walk in a significant measure of transparency before God and each other in this age. In this way, they can be immune from all attacks of sorcery and witchcraft because manipulation, intimidation, and rebellion or misuse of authority is a thing of the past. Overcoming the roots of witchcraft is both a personal and a group decision that all must embrace-beginning with the leadership of the group whether the group is 5 or 5,000 people.

PART IV:

OUR FIGHT FOR
THE SAKE OF OTHERS

10

CONTENDING FOR COMMUNITY WHOLENESS AND HEALTH

In the last few chapters, we have been looking at the use of our spiritual authority and the need to overcoming witchcraft at the root-level. God has given us access to tremendous power and authority to heal the sick, cast out demons, and even raise the dead. Indeed, God wants to pour out the release of healing power like we have not yet seen on the earth.

However, the exercise of spiritual authority and overcoming the roots of witchcraft is both a personal and a group decision that we all must embrace. The leadership must set the pace in choosing the wisdom of God over the wisdom of satan. Embracing God's wisdom corporately is a key to community wholeness and even personal health.

Who are WE to God?

In chapters 4 through 6 we looked at our personal identity in Christ. Within the American culture we emphasize our individual identity in Christ. However, in the American culture we tend neglect the importance of the corporate *who we are* to Jesus. The scripture says that we are the Bride of Christ, The House of Prayer, God's temple, God's family, and the Body of Christ. Jesus also described us as a city on a hill. Our brothers in China and Africa have a much better understanding and importance of our corporate identity in Jesus Christ.

As the Bride of Christ, we corporately have access to the deep things that are in the heart of God for us. God has invited us to understand what makes Him glad. God has also invited us corporately into garden of Gethsemane to know what causes His heart to ache. Knowing the deep things of God is our glorious inheritance forever. God is leading us individually and corporately with all of us in mind.

We are also the army of God- Jesus is the Lord of hosts. Most armies bring destruction, death, and sorrow wherever they march. Under the Captain of the Hosts of Heaven, the Bride of Christ is to march forth and bring redemption, life, and joy wherever we go. All of creation is waiting for this "army" to march and bring healing to the nations.

As God's temple, Jesus is still building us as individual living stones. God has also sent master builders commissioned by Jesus to build up the Church as gifts to his people-like the apostle Paul. Like any other building project, discipleship of individuals, communities, and nations take time, physical resources, and labor.

We are also the house of prayer. Forever, we will behold the majesty, kindness and goodness of God together and respond with worship. In this age and the next, we also get rule with Jesus forever through speaking His decrees back to the Father (also called prayer) under the anointing of the Holy Spirit. History began with a prayer meeting in Genesis 1 and in Revelation 22 (after satan is vanquished), it ends in a prayer meeting.

As the house of prayer for nations, we will not be complete until every tongue, tribe, and ethnic group is part of us. Jesus gave the great commission and meant it. God is looking for a dwelling place made of people from every tongue, tribe, and people group in deep agreement with Him.

Jesus called us a "city on a hill". Cities were places of refuge and resource to weary settlers in biblical times. We are to be a place where broken people can come and find refuge and restoration. Even as Jesus is working to make all things new in us- we can then turn around and do the same thing to build and bless other people.

We are also a global family affection. God is our Father. Jesus is our elder brother. Within the family, there are "spiritual fathers and mothers" with maturity to build up and train others. God is bringing together people of diverse cultures and circumstances to love each other as a sign and wonder on the earth.

The Church in Corinth- broken with much carnality

Paul planted the Church in Corinth-a city infested with immorality, pagan temples, and other ills. The power of the Holy Spirit began sweeping through the city and a fair number of people came to Jesus as the result. Sometime later, Paul began to get troubling reports from others on his team combined with the letters that the Corinthian leaders were writing to Paul. However, Paul wrote:

In the following directives I have no praise for you, for your meetings do more harm than good. (1 Corinthians 11:17)

In essence Paul is saying, don't meet together until you get the following problems fixed. Can you imagine a local pastor saying something like this on a Sunday morning? What was it?

From other passages in 1 Corinthians, we find that there were issues of sexual immorality (1 Corinthians 6), confusion around Christian freedom (1 Corinthians 8-10), false teaching related to the resurrection (1 Corinthians 15) and disorder in the midst of worship (1 Corinthians 12-14). However, we don't find as scathing rebuke as in 1 Corinthians 11:17.

From the scriptural and cultural context, we find that there were both the rich and the poor in the city. At least once a week, they would gather to worship Jesus and enjoy a meal together-a "love feast". The rich would get to the meeting early and bringing their great wealth of food and share it with each other.

Meanwhile, the poor "working class" would get off work late and end up getting to the meeting late. Often they would need to skip meals simply because they didn't have enough money to eat. The church gathering for the "love feast" was perhaps their one chance every week to have a good meal.

However, the rich early-comers were not waiting for poor late-comers. Instead, the late-comers were left to eat the crumbs of what the rich had left for them. While they were eating, the rich were waiting for what was next on the agenda for the evening meeting. The underlying message is that they were a burden instead of a blessing. Paul wrote of the situation:

When you come together, it is not the Lord's Supper that you eat, for as you eat, each of you goes ahead without waiting for anybody else. One remains hungry, another gets drunk. Don't you have homes to eat and drink in? Or do you despise the church of God and humiliate those who have nothing? What shall I say to you? Shall I praise you for this? Certainly not! (1 Corinthians 11:20-23)

Even as the services are supposed to highlight the corporate unity and love between everyone in the Body of Christ, the net result was the opposite.

The gatherings highlighted the division, strife, and oppression of the poor (a sign of arrogance). Instead of healthy soul ties of humility, honor, and righteousness within the community, the human interactions were producing bitterness and shame. As the result, the whole church was experiencing the discipline of God where people were getting sick and even physically dying in a premature way.

Understanding our "soul" and the power of the soul-ties:

God made humanity with three parts: spirit, soul, and body. Before the fall in the garden, our spirit man could interact with the supernatural freely. Our physical bodies could interact freely with the physical material realm. Our soul (consisting of our mind, emotions, and our will) could easily interact our spirit and body and make decisions. When we ate from the tree of the knowledge of good and evil, and severed pure communion with God, God removed the ability to easily communicate and interact with the supernatural realm to slow the destructive process of sin. To those who are born again, God allows believers to experience two-way communication with Him through the Holy Spirit. Physical death occurs when our soul becomes separated from our physical bodies.

When we gave our lives over to Jesus, the Holy Spirit came in and dwells within our human spirit. God will communicate truth to our spirit by the Holy Spirit and we will know it in our soul. In this way we can interact with the supernatural realm. We also interact with the physical realm with our bodies- and with other people at both the physical level and emotional level. Paul told us to be transformed by the renewing of our mind, and to submit our physical bodies as living sacrifices (Romans 12:1-2). This happens when we submit our soul and body to the Holy Spirit that dwells within our human spirit to what we know is Jesus' desires and wisdom for our lives.

In relating to people, we gain an affection in the soul for the ones we enjoy being with. Over time, we get to interacting with people on a deeper, emotional level than simply being with them physically or doing stuff with them. A "soul tie" or emotional bond forms between the people. We can deeply influence and affect each other for good or for bad. Scripture warns us to be careful with friendship (Pro.12:26, 18:24, 22:24 etc.) because of this dynamic.

Even after we are born-again, satan will use deep "soul ties" with our interpersonal relationships to attempt to influence us away from following Jesus. If the enemy cannot directly attack us, he will attempt to hurt the people around us by causing bitterness to get into their souls. This is why a root of bitterness in one can defile many (Hebrews 12:15). Satan desires to control our will through our soul: our mind, and our emotions in reaction to physical things-and get access to our spirit bodies.

Due to the dynamics related to soul ties, some types of prayer can actually do more damage than good. Soulish "prayers" based on bitterness or to control someone (usually justified because of the "obvious arrogance" of the person) can really hurt people emotionally and even physically. They constitute a misuse of our spiritual authority in Jesus Christ. Sadly, I've seen many instances of this. In these cases, satan does not need to directly attack most groups of believers through sorcery through witches, warlocks, and shamans.

Often the "prayers" of misguided and offended believers work just as well in satan's purposes. I've sat and counseled many people in the midst of ministry who feel oppressed. In interviewing them, I would find out that they had been hit by "friendly fire" or "charismatic witchcraft" that was contrary to the will of God revealed in scripture. Here are some signs of attack from enemy witchcraft or "friendly fire" due to an unhealthy soul tie:

1. A feeling of depression, oppression, or hopeless in the midst of neutral or favorable circumstances.
2. An inability to think rationally- as if under the influence of "mind-control".
3. Enhanced amounts of temptation, especially in the area of sexual immorality.
4. An upset stomach, severe headaches, and a general "ill" feeling that suddenly came on for no reason.
5. After breaking the soul-tie through the name of Jesus, and renouncing any type of spiritual attack, the person suddenly recovers "on the spot".

This illustrates is how important it is to maintain deep unity and love with other Christians. In the Corinthian Church, the arrogance, humiliation of the poor, broken relationships, and division allowed satan to use these toxic soul ties to bring sickness and death (1 Corinthians 11:27-30).

Often in the midst of deliverance ministry sessions, I will ask the person to "break off" unhealthy soul times (former boy friends, girl friends, teachers etc.). I will then ask them to bless those who really hurt them with their words. If the person is sincere before God, the result often an immediate healing as Truth is exalted.

Soul ties are a significant issue- as we are the body of Christ and connected to each other deeply and relationally. In the case of the Corinthian church a culture of dishonor was bringing harm to the individual believers. However, a culture of honor (like in Acts 4) brings tremendous healing and gives a powerful witness to the entire region.

Needed: A culture of Honor

So what does it take to build a culture of honor like this? I believe scripture gives us some very important hints:

1. A commitment to forgive others and cover them.

Since we still live in a broken world and we are still being saved, sin is almost inevitable. In the midst of community, we inevitably discover each other's brokenness and weakness and it hurts. Our natural reaction is bitterness and anger because we got hurt by other people. The trust level of other people drops- what now?

Jesus commanded us to forgive, calling it an eternal life issue (Matthew 6:14-15). On the other hand, if we refuse to forgive, it is an open invitation for demonic oppression to come and feast on our bitterness. Medical studies have shown that many physical illnesses and diseases are related to the inability to forgive and move on.

Meanwhile, forgiving and then covering those who hurt us often brings healing. Often the other guy is hurting as God has "cut" them with the conviction of the Holy Spirit. Often when people forgive and then bless those who hurt them, friendships are restored and the power of the Holy Spirit flows in greater measure. James 5 links confession, and forgiving others with a greater release of healing power.

2. No gossip or slander allowed!

The Apostle James gave a long discourse on the use of the tongue in James 3. We can't effectively both bless God in spirit and truth while at the same time using our tongue to slander and hurt other people. The book of Proverbs also talks much about the use of our words.

The tongue has the power of life and death, and those who love it will eat its fruit. (Proverbs 18:21)

God has given incredible people incredible delegated power in our words. We need to use them wisely and with great honor.

However, the Body of Christ has a paralyzing disease called "foot and mouth disease". We do the equivalent of sticking our foot in our mouths when we gossip and slander other members in the Body of Christ. We often talk about each other behind their back in ways that we would never talk about them if they were present. To compound the problem, we don't view it as seriously as sexual immorality or financial impropriety. It's often viewed as being "cool" or insightful.

The problem with gossip is that it destroys the trust factor within a community. Let's say that at the "First Church of Dysfunctional Relationships", "Sister Susie" has a problem with Brother Andrew. Sister Susie goes and tells everyone else in her circle of friends. Meanwhile, Sister Trisha has an issue with Sister Susie who is in the group listening. Sister Trisha is now encouraged to tell everyone about the problem she has with Sister Susie. For a moment, Sister Trisha's social status within the group has increased for leaking the "juicy" details.

However, what has happened to the group is that a culture of mistrust has formed where people cannot be transparent and safe to each other. Let's say that someone else in the group that we will call "Sister Anne" has a problem that is causing her to be depressed. She most likely won't go to the Church for help with her problem because she fears that her embarrassing "dirty laundry" will become the latest gossip news like Sister Susie's troubles. As the result, bondage in Sister Anne's life grows because her original problem is now compounded because she cannot trust the Church of Jesus Christ to provide a solution without her getting humiliated.

Many of our local prayer meetings are simply gossip sessions with our eyes closed and the name of "Jesus" slapped on it. "We need to pray for Sister Susie and Brother Andrew because_____". Satan and his demons actually enjoy "prayer" meetings like this. Meanwhile we wonder why the Body of Jesus Christ does not manifest authority in prayer to heal the sick, cast out demons, and raise the dead.

3. A commitment to settle disputes and confront sin according to Matthew 18:15-20 and other passages of scripture.

Many simple disputes explode into destructive conflicts that destroy the local Church simply because they are not dealt with in a biblically centered way. Most of the time, we want a dispute settled because we were wronged and we want justice from the other guy (even if it comes at the expense of the rest of the Body of Christ). Instead of going to the people we have an issue with, we then go out and tell everyone else our side of the story and why the other guy is wrong. People are now taking sides over the conflict. What originated as a simple conflict between individuals has now exploded into a corporate conflict and now threatens to split the local congregation. Meanwhile, non-Christians look at this and then look elsewhere to get their problems taken care of.

It takes a vigorous spirituality to settle a dispute in a godly way with the end goal of greater unity within the Body of Christ, and the supremacy of Jesus is exalted. It may mean that the original damage personally suffered does not get immediately fixed. This type of "conflict resolution" when injury was involved is impossible to redress unless we understand that Jesus is a just judge and that he is for us. Can the Judge of the earth not make wrong things right?

Underlying any type of conflict is the need to trust in the sovereignty of God- God specifically allowed you to get wronged as he could have easily prevented the trouble. Is God not able to restore what was lost? In the midst of conflicting parties, satan has an agenda to bring destruction while God has an agenda to build the Body of Christ and bring life.

4. A commitment to walk in Truth with each other

Where the picture gets messy is when sin is involved. We are all weak and broken people. Human dynamics come into play as well. It is difficult and painful to admit to others that we fell short, knowing that others could decide that the "remedy" is unpleasant and costly. As the result, it is often much easier to not confess sin into the light which allows it to grow.

Unrepentant sin within the Body of Christ is also a serious issue. If a corporate Body of Christ embraces those in unrepentant sin, it will inevitably grieve the Holy Spirit and cause disruption in our individual and corporate fellowship with God. We have seen the destruction that run-away sin has caused related to the sexual abuse scandals that we have heard of lately.

The Apostle Paul rebuked the Church in Corinth for celebrating open scandalous sin in the name of "freedom" in 1 Corinthians 6. Instead, Paul commanded the church to put the man who was involved in the scandalous sin and refused to repent out of their fellowship. Removing someone from fellowship due to defiant sin should be a swift warning that they are in danger of falling away and losing their eternal salvation. Numerous biblical passages warn that those who live in unrepentant sin will not go to heaven. Unprotected by the prayers of other followers of Jesus, they are now more exposed to the attacks of the enemy including sickness.

5. A commitment to believe the best about each other and to fight on behalf of each other:

However, removing someone from fellowship is practically not a big penalty unless there are deep relational bonds and a deep commitment to honor each other by fighting for each other. Paul wrote in 1 Corinthians 12:

The eye cannot say to the hand, "I don't need you!" And the head cannot say to the feet, "I do not need you!" On the contrary, those parts of the body that seem to be weaker are

indispensable, and the parts that we think are less honorable we treat with special honor.(1 Corinthians 12:21-24)

In fighting for each other and honoring each other in spirit and truth, we become an impregnable wall for the enemy to infiltrate the Church to harm us. In addition, when there is a commitment to honor and fight for each other in prayer, humility, and servant-hood; a dynamic synergy is produced where the whole is much greater than the sum of the parts.

Many people have been struggling with sin patterns for years. They are secure in Christ as they repent, hate the sin, and fight against it, but they cannot break free. The sin is not simply a personal problem, but it is a community problem.

Therefore confess your sins to each other and pray for each other so that you may be healed. The prayer of a righteous man is powerful and effective. (James 5:16)

In the case of someone who is repentant, but simply cannot break free, what is the community going to do? In some cases, the brokenness is so deep that only the community together can bring healing and restoration. Often it is a major battle that may expose weaknesses of the whole community that Jesus is trying to address.

Sadly, most of the time, the Body of Christ simply shuns the person and walks away from the shame of the guy not being able to overcome it. As the result, the whole community misses an opportunity for breakthrough in corporate humility and victory. The corporate problems Jesus wanted to deal with through bringing healing are often left unaddressed.

Meanwhile, Jesus promised that he would build the church and even the strongest bondages could not stop Him. In the midst of the breakthrough, the community is often brought closer together in love and humility. When "unbreakable" bondage gets overcome by the power of God expressed in community, there is often corporate breakthrough and great joy.

The promise of healing in community:

One of the major biblical promises in scripture is related to healing. God first revealed himself to the Jewish people as is the LORD who heals his people in Exodus 15:26. Scripture says that there was not one feeble among all of Israel (Psalm 105:37-38) after being slaves in Egypt for centuries. After King Hezekiah prayed in the first Passover celebrated in many years, God responded by healing the people (2 Chronicles 30:20)-ALL of them.

Under the old covenant, Jesus also healed all the people on occasion. Thanks to Jesus' sacrificial death on the cross and then resurrection, we live under a renewed covenant with better promises and greater grace available. Paul writes:

Now if the ministry that brought death, which was engraved in letters on stone, came with glory, so that the Israelites could not look steadily at the face of Moses because of its glory, fading though it was, will not the ministry of the Spirit be even more glorious? If the ministry that condemns men is glorious, how much more glorious is the ministry that brings righteousness! (2 Corinthians 3:7-9)

In the days before Jesus returns, there will be places where ALL get healed, regardless of physical condition.

Jesus Christ is still the head of the Church. However, Jesus is in heaven communicating with us by the power of the Holy Spirit. It also means that He is not on earth. Thus we were meant to be the continuation of Jesus' ministry on the earth. When we dwell together, united in love and humility- it becomes an open invitation for the Holy Spirit to come in power and rest upon a community.

For example, in a community led by Dave and Ivy Anderson called "Acts 29", God had put it on our hearts to send a teenager named "Kim" dealing with brokenness to Awakening Teen Camp. The camp is a 10-day program put on by IHOP-KC for teenagers to encounter God, make commitments to Jesus, and get raised up to influence their peers and high schools for the Kingdom of God. It would take several hundred dollars for her to go to camp- money that no individual had. In addition, her parents were also opposed to Kim going.

We did a number of fund-raising projects including "change for change". The concept was simple. All of us would save the pennies, nickels, dimes, and quarters that we get and save them. All of that money would then add up. In answer to prayer, her parents yielded and suddenly Kim was off to awakening Teen camp.

However, the story does not end there- at the camp, Kim had a heavenly encounter with Jesus where she saw the throne of God. She knew the love of Jesus at a deeper level than before. Kim came back and testified to what happened at the teen camp in the Acts 29 gathering and the power of God came into the room. Several people were healed that night including one young man with a serious heart condition. In the midst of the unity and love through the name of Jesus for the sake of the broken, the Holy Spirit came in power and people were healed.

11

SPIRITUAL WARFARE OVER RESOURCES AND WEALTH

Money- we talk about it all the time. We love it, we hate it. One song says that "Money makes the world go 'round". Money is a common medium to express the value of our individual resources, time spent, physical labor, and our ideas. Obviously, the value we put on certain resources and ideas is different than what the next guy thinks.

By looking at the checkbooks of most American Christians, I can tell what the primary values of our culture are. Based upon how we spend our discretionary income (after food, base-line sheltering needs, and basic clothing needs). Our top values include: 1.) Looking good to impress other people. 2.) Keeping ourselves entertained. 3.) Maintaining our physical health and comfort. 4. Overspending on ourselves- even if it at the expense of generations after us. Where is building the Kingdom of God on the list? Jesus warned:

For where your treasure is, there your heart will be also. (Matthew 6:21)

Meanwhile, we wonder why the Church in the United States (and the West) is so often lukewarm with lots of bondage.

Sadly, fights about money and resource allocation have ruined more than one outreach and divided more than one local Church. Many times, resource allocation is done based on politics in the local church instead of seeking God for information on how He wants resources allocated. Meanwhile, people who don't know Jesus or are now offended at the church believe all that the Church wants is money. We need a return to some basic biblical economics on the individual level. Then we need to look corporately:

Biblical economics 101

There are over 2,000 scripture verses that address the topic of wealth, money, and resources. There are far more scripture verses on wealth than on prayer! Thus the topic of wealth and resources must be important to God. As covered in chapter 3, God is going to bring the heavens (supernatural realms) and the earth (physical material realm) together under the leadership of Jesus. Wealth and resources are also important to satan, because he offered Jesus all the wealth and the glories of the kingdoms of the world in exchange for worship.

First, we need to understand that God owns it all. Genesis tells us that God created the heavens and the earth. Ultimately everything on the earth is the Lord's. Since God created it all by His own voice and power, God therefore inherently owns it all.

Second, even though creation is broken under the effects of sin, we can still see that God is incredibly wise and generous. The reason the wicked often currently prosper is not because God is passive. It is because God is incredibly kind to all people. Jesus said of enemies:

But I tell you: Love your enemies and pray for those who persecute you, that you may be sons of your Father in heaven. He causes his sun to rise on the evil and the good, and sends rain on the righteous and the unrighteous. (Matthew 5:44-45)

All of us were once enemies with God until God graciously turned our hearts back to Him through Jesus Christ, canceling our debt by the blood of Jesus.

Third, if God ultimately owns it all- it means that we ultimately do not own anything. Ultimately we are servants and stewards of everything on God's earth as human beings. It means that we are accountable to God for what we do with the physical resources and wealth on the earth.

Forth, the Bible presents wealth as a blessing, while poverty is a curse. The first covenant curses in Deuteronomy 28:15-19 for corporate disobedience are economic troubles and the drying up of the production of wealth. The enemy has been able to lie to the Church that being poor is a key to becoming "more pleasing to God" or "more spiritual". Through this lie, the enemy has been able to keep wealth in the hands of the wicked that oppress the poor. God wants to put wealth into the hands of people who will not be corrupted by it and will use it to bring good news to the poor.

Fifth, wealth is a great servant but a horrible taskmaster. Wealth is important, but it is not the end goal. Attempting to gain and then use greater physical resources for kingdom purposes only one of the ways to worship and honor Jesus. Jesus warned that we could not both serve God and mammon in Matthew 6:24. Behind mammon are demonic spirits of greed and materialism. Paul warned:

For the love of money is a root of all kinds of evil. Some people, eager for money, have wandered from the faith and pierced themselves with many griefs. (1Timothy 6:10)

The devil promises pleasure and power in an all-out pursuit of wealth. In the pursuit of wealth, other things are sacrificed such as intimacy with God, and building godly family. Then when the wealth arrives, its benefits are far less than what was promised. In pursuing wealth and resources at the expense of time with Jesus, gaining wisdom, and building godly relationships, so many American families have opened themselves up to the attack and the oppression of the enemy.

Biblically, prosperity is defined as wholeness (relationally, emotionally, physically, and spiritually) and having basic needs met in abundance so that we can be a blessing to other people. Biblical prosperity is more about what we can give away for the glory of God than receive. The Bible gives a lot of insight into how to gain godly wealth and wholeness based upon the book of Proverbs and the Sermon on the Mount. Some basic biblical principles are: 1.) Be diligent. 2.) Be faithful. 3.) Gain Wisdom and knowledge; it's worth spending resources to acquire this. 4.) Practice righteousness and justice. 5.) Take Sabbath rest- money isn't everything. 6.) Use the resources to serve and bless others. 7.) Bring the tithe and offerings to God- it's the only way to show the LORD that we are not in bondage to materialism. 8.) Do not be anxious, but trust that God is good and generous.

Blessings or curses: Do we stand with God's ancient people and plan?

There are natural things to enhance our ability to gather wealth. Many other books have been written in the world and within the Church related to finances. However, scripture also talks about invisible, spiritual factors that also determine how much wealth an individual or group of people are entrusted with. We can see in society that God gives some people greater physical, relational, and intellectual abilities than others. God gives different gifts to different people.

The same is true related to physical wealth-God gives some individuals, groups, and nations of people power to make wealth for the sake of confirming the covenant (Deuteronomy 8:18). For example, God chose Abraham and then his offspring (Isaac, and Jacob) to have the primary leadership role in world redemption.

The LORD had said to Abram, "Leave your country, your people and your father's household and go to the land I will show you. "I will make you into a great nation and I will bless you; I will make your name great, and you will be a blessing. I will bless those who bless you and whoever curses you I will curse; and all peoples on earth will be blessed through you." (Genesis 12:1-3)

Though in general, the Jewish people have not been faithful to their national calling, God continues to be faithful to the descendents of Abraham, Isaac, and Jacob. Jesus said he will not return to the earth until the Jewish people welcome him back (Matthew 23:37-39).

Indeed, if someone were to follow the wealth and power of empires throughout history, those that blessed and protected Israel were blessed with leadership among the Gentile nations. However, nations or empires that cursed or betrayed Israel ended up under the judgment of God. Nationally and individually, anti-Semitism brings a curse. Those who hate the Jews are ignorantly opposing God's plan for world-redemption. Sadly, the church has often been tricked by satan and his demonic hordes to do just that.

On the other hand, standing with God's heart for the oppressed (Isaiah 58:6-12) and His eternal plan for world redemption brings a tremendous blessing. God promised the Jewish people through the prophet Isaiah:

I have posted watchmen on your walls, O Jerusalem, they will never be silent day or night. You who call on the LORD, give yourselves no rest, and give him no rest till he establishes Jerusalem and makes her the praise of the earth. (Isaiah 62:6-7)

God promised the Jewish people, that He would establish watchmen in Israel and other nations who would remind the LORD of His promises until God fulfilled his plan for world redemption and make Jerusalem a center of blessing to the whole earth. Practically speaking, it will take physical resources to train and set the watchmen on the wall. Anyone who partners with what God is doing ends up under the blessing of God-including power to be a greater blessing.

Jesus went further on the Sermon on the Mount. In speaking to His Jewish brethren related to worry and finances he said:

But seek first his kingdom and his righteousness, and all these things will be given to you as well. Therefore do not worry about tomorrow, for tomorrow will worry about itself. Each day has enough trouble of its own. (Matthew 6:33-34)

The author of Hebrews later wrote:

May the God of peace, who through the blood of the eternal covenant brought back from the dead our Lord Jesus, that great Shepherd of the sheep, equip you with everything good for doing his will, and may he work in us what is pleasing to him, through Jesus Christ, to whom be glory for ever and ever. Amen. (Hebrews 13:20-21)

Clearly, God is tying His blessing to partnership with Him through words and deeds to build the Church, fulfill the great commission, and provoking the Jewish people to inviting their Messiah back to rule and reign. The passages are clearly saying that if we do God's vision using God's wisdom and ways, we will stay under the blessing of God including financial resources. We can't out-give God, but it's the one area that God gives us permission to "test" Him in.

Exposing the hidden spiritual warfare related to believers acquiring wealth:

I have heard many stories about believers who were selfish and passive and not agreement with the things that are deeply on God's heart. However, by the grace of God, they were suddenly awakened to the passion in God's heart for them. With burning hearts, they set out to know how to love Jesus. In seeking more of Jesus, they eventually run into God's kingdom purposes related to bringing the gospel to every ethnic group including Israel. They then take action related to their wealth and resources. However, they then came under attack in their finances and in other ways once they took decisive action. Why?

We need to understand that satan and demons are happy with passive "believers" of Jesus-even if they have wealth. However, satan is fearful of whole-hearted, deeply committed disciples of Jesus acquiring wealth. More resources in the hands of deeply committed disciples of Jesus means more anointed, trained workers serving to bring the gospel to un-reached people groups. More riches mean more souls in the Kingdom of God. More wealth means more "watchmen on the wall" who pray day and night for Israel to be saved. It also means more intercessors to strike blows against the enemy blinding un-reached people groups. Therefore, satan hates the acquisition of wealth by godly people- his kingdom on the earth is at stake.

One of the primary ways the enemy either attacks newly awakened believers with wealth or contests the release of resources to passionate believers in Jesus is to accuse the saints before heaven related to deep sin in generations past. God warned against idolatry and its related curse that would affect generations to come:

You shall not make for yourself an idol in the form of anything in heaven above or on the earth beneath or in the waters below. You shall not bow down to them or worship them; for I, the LORD your God, am a jealous God, punishing the children for the sins of the fathers to the third and fourth generation of those who hate me, but showing love to a thousand generations of those who love me and keep my commandments. (Exodus 20:4-6)

The apostle James picked up the theme in James 4:4-5 related to the warning against materialism. So we can conclude that idolatry (including materialism) and sorcery (interaction with demons) brings a curse that negatively affects the generations.

In Deuteronomy 27, Moses also gave another list of particularly grievous sins that bring a curse upon people. The list begins with idolatry (verse 15). The list then moves on to dishonoring parents and other acts of injustice particularly related to the vulnerable (verses 16-19), abominations related to sexual immorality (verses 20-23), murder (verses 24-25) and it ends with idolatry in the form of rebellion (verse 26). Other passages warn of sins that bring a curse including priests abusing their offices (Malachi 1:12-2:9) and robbing God in the area of tithes and offerings (Malachi 3:1-12).

In Deuteronomy 28:15-68, God warned the nation of Israel related to the covenant curses that would touch them nationally if they forsook the LORD and went after other gods. One of the first curses mentioned in verses 15-20 is judgments related to economics. In Genesis 4, God cursed Cain's ability to produce anything of value from his labor as a judgment for killing Abel. Thanks be to Jesus Christ who has redeemed us from the curse.

From Exodus 20 we are warned that such curses can affect generations to come as well. Satan and his demons claim that the sins of the fathers give him a legal right to oppress the godly offspring- and contest the release of resources for Kingdom purposes. (Satan ignores passages such as Ezekiel 18 about individual responsibility in searching for "rights" to oppress people.)

However, Jesus took the curse so we could be grafted into the covenant blessings of God to Abraham's offspring. In Christ we are citizens of the commonwealth of Israel. In this case, we must use our authority in Jesus Christ to break the curses of the enemy and unlock the resources of the earth for Kingdom purposes.

Unlimited budget from heaven available- if we do God's work, God's way.

Satanic wisdom has started many church fights and ruined many Kingdom of God initiatives over money. One of the key lies the enemy uses: *There's not enough money or resources to do everything that is on God's heart.* Worldly economics 101 tells us that there are only so many scarce resources, and individuals or groups need to strategize on how to use these scarce resources.

Biblical economics 101 tells us that God created everything through simply speaking and He now owns everything (seen and unseen). What this means is instead of fighting for our ministry's right to a slice of the resources, we can use the wisdom of God to prefer and honor other ministries within a local congregation who also have biblical kingdom initiatives. If it is very important to God and the right timing for our ministry plan, God will inspire people to give and release resources-even in some unexpected ways.

Since God owns it all, we should not need to stress over an apparent lack of funding or resources. If we are doing God's visions using God's righteous wisdom (including the honoring other groups within the local church with Jesus-centered kingdom initiatives), it's now God's "problem" to release resources since the government rests upon the shoulders of Jesus.

For example, in the spring of 2013- IHOP-KC was part of the Global Outreach Day (G.O.D.) that encouraged everyone to reach out to their neighbors with the love of Jesus. IHOP-KC was also facing huge budget constraints and many other departments were doing very important things. Mike Bickle gave an impossible assignment to the Evangelism department: With a $5,000 budget and 40 days to get ready, bring together an outreach to bless the city of Grandview with hopes of reaching 2,000 people.

Laurie Ditto was chosen as the primary leader and organizer for this massive undertaking. Laurie Ditto's first reaction was, "God, HELP!" Laurie got together a leadership team that would pray. The team began to pray and seek the face of God for favor while working to secure the logistics of the outreach- who would be on stage presenting the gospel? Who would do the music, food, security, bounce houses and other games for the kids, first aid, and a raffle with prizes? Also, there was no "Plan B" if it rained on May 25th.

Then there was the issue of inviting a whole rather skeptical city to the party. Many people in Grandview and the greater Kansas City area had a rather suspicious and unfavorable view of IHOP-KC due to various controversies over 30 years. The small leadership team continued to pray and do lots of research on where everyone lived. The goal would be to visit every house the weekend of May 18th and invite that household to the party on May 25th.

The hand of God was evident early on in the process. On May 3rd, a freak snowstorm cancelled all of the government celebrations for the city of Grandview. It was one of the latest snows in KC history. God then brought together 20 other ministry leaders together in unity. Glad Heart Reality offered an additional $2,000 to bless Grandview. Then a sanitation company donated $880 worth of Porta-Potties freely for the day.

Some were still skeptical as the final week turned into a time scramble. There were last minute changes that needed to be made. Many on the leadership team worked 12 or more hours a day as an extravagant offering of time to Jesus. With far less volunteers than what had been hoped for, the team was able to visit 90% of the households in Grandview the week of May 18th to May 24th.

Suddenly as the event neared, thousands of other dollars worth of resources were offered for the sake of celebrating Grandview. The fire department and police department showed up to reach out to kids. The city fast-tracked permit applications and waived the fee two days before the event- something that normally take more than two weeks to get approved.

The weather forecast was ominous: rain and thunderstorms were likely on the Saturday of the outreach. However, God had given this outreach all this favor- would He now prevent the children from hearing the good news of Jesus? God answered one last push of intense corporate intercession for the event and shifted the jet stream the day of the outreach. The thunderstorm complex was diverted into Iowa.

That afternoon, roughly 2,000 people from the community enjoyed celebrating Grandview and hearing the love of Jesus proclaimed. Dozens made decisions to follow Jesus. An outreach that should have cost $25,000 or more was done with an initial budget of $5,000. In doing God's work God's way (with humility, wisdom, and excellence), we had entered into God's economy of unlimited supply and then God had done the impossible.

117

12

FIGHTING FOR THE ONES WE LOVE

"Believe in the Lord Jesus and you will be saved- you and your household." (Acts 16:31)

On a Friday morning, an older couple entered a ministry room set up for prophetic ministry. They are asking the Lord for a specific prophetic word. As they sit down and I explain how the prophetic ministry teams work at IHOP-KC work, I could sense the heaviness upon their hearts.

After I prayed, the Holy Spirit immediately highlighted their son. As I ask them whether they have a son that is running from God, this beautiful couple burst into tears. The ministry time concluded with a prayer agreeing with their desire to see their son turn to the Lord for salvation, asking God for perseverance in prayer and loving him until he get turned back. As a minister of the Gospel and an intercessory missionary, I see this way too often.

From a sociological point of view, the Church in America appears to be dying. For the generation before World War II, roughly 60% of the population regularly attended Church on Sunday. With the Baby-boomer generation, the percentage of people who regularly attend church drops to 35%. For Generation "X" or the Baby Buster generation, the number drops to less than 15%. For the digital generation, the number is less than 5%. In many churches, there are only older, grey heads in the pews- no young people. Many churches are simply forced to close their doors. Is there anything that can be done to reverse the tide? Does God even care?

Jesus came to seek and save the lost:

Jesus has always had us on his mind. When Adam and Eve sinned against God by eating from the Tree of the Knowledge of Good and Evil, it did not change that reality. In Genesis 3, it says that God sent his angel to guard the way to the Tree of Life. John describes Jesus Christ as the Lamb of God slain from the foundation of the world. From eternity past, it has always been in the heart for God to rescue the broken.

The prophetic books are all about God's burning desire for His people to return. The people have gone astray after other gods- greatly grieving the Holy one of Israel. Through the prophet Ezekiel he cried out,

Therefore, O house of Israel, I will judge you, each one according to his ways, declares the Sovereign LORD. Repent! Turn away from all your offenses; then sin will not be your downfall. Rid yourselves of all the offenses you have committed and get a new heart and a new spirit. Why will you die, O house of Israel? For I take no pleasure in the death of anyone, declares the Sovereign LORD. Repent and live! (Ezekiel 18:30-32)

Yet the people refused to turn back to the Lord.

When Jesus walked on the earth, he never turned away any person who was sincerely seeking Him. Everyone in scripture that sought out Jesus sincerely got their sins forgiven and/or their bodies healed. The only ones He got really angry at were the religious leaders of Israel- why? Jesus gave us an indicator of why.

Woe to you, experts in the law, because you have taken away the key of knowledge. You yourselves have not entered, and you have hindered those who were entering. (Luke 11:52)

The religious leaders should have known better related to the coming Messiah. However, due to their stubborn conceit, self-centeredness at the expense of others, and hypocrisy, they were more concerned about the traditions of men than caring for the people. As the result, they were blocking people from coming to know Jesus.

Jesus told a series of parables in Luke 15 related to his desire to bring us into the Kingdom of righteousness. The parable of the lost coin and the parable of the lost sheep describe Jesus' joy over one sinner who turns back to righteousness. The parable of the pearl of great price describes how Jesus feels about one person (the pearl) in the midst of the field (the sea of humanity). Jesus purchased our salvation at the cross for all of humanity because He had you in mind.

The parable of the prodigal son tells us how far God will pursue us as a Father. The prodigal son asks for his share of the inheritance immediately. In Jewish culture he would get the inheritance only when his father died. In essence, this son was saying, "Drop dead dad!" A Jewish father could have this young man stoned for rebellion and insolence. Yet in the parable, the father gave his son what he wished. In heart-ache, God will often give those without Christ what they want- knowing it will hurt them in the long-term.

Not surprisingly, he went off and squandered it on wild living in the parable. He then found himself as a hired hand, feeding slop to the pigs. To a young Jewish man, this was the ultimate insult as pigs were considered "unclean" to the Jewish people. In the midst of hitting rock-bottom, he came to his senses and eventually walked back home.

Yet the parable continues in that the father was looking for him. When he saw him, he ran out to get the best robe, and ring, and told the servants to throw a party for him. God the Father welcomed him back. Jesus celebrates the return of His sons and daughters- even if they come back in pretty bad shape, having lost everything. What about you?

Jesus is the Desire of the nations- but the lost don't want our traditions or religion.

In the Book of Revelation, John presents a scene that we all want to be a part of- people standing before God unashamed with everything in plain view. From every tongue, tribe, people group and nation they are worshipping the One who paid such a high price to save his people. The prophet Haggai says of Jesus:

"This is what the LORD Almighty says: 'In a little while, I will once more shake the heavens and the earth, the sea and the dry land. I will shake all the nations and the desired of all nations will come and I will fill this house with glory' says the LORD Almighty."(Haggai 2:6-7)

Jesus is called the desire of the nations- people from every culture in the earth will love Him. When young, old, male, and female meet Jesus today with an encounter, they wanted to follow Him all of their days. Yet for many younger people, to put up a "Church" sign is a good way to make them stay away. What is the disconnect?

As noted earlier, what really angered Jesus the most were the religious leaders who were fake- and operating from a religious spirit. A practical definition of "religion" is simply doing my own thing (which is usually not good), but then attaching the name of God to it as if it was divine truth. In extreme cases, murder is justified because they are doing "god" a service.

People like this actually have nothing to do with Jesus. Satan loves to use this tactic to cause both Jews and Gentiles to be repulsed by the hypocrisy. Those who are in deliberate agreement with this are in big trouble with Jesus- He compares people like this to "wolves" and has reserved the worst torments of hell for them if they do not repent.

Even if we are not in deliberate agreement with this malevolent strategy of satan, the enemy still uses a religious spirit to get local congregations "stuck in a rut" and makes them ineffective. Something that began as genuine activity of the Holy Spirit can turn into culture and tradition that hinders people from coming into the Kingdom. What God was blessing and anointing ten years ago may not be what God is blessing and anointing today. Jesus is constantly doing new things in the earth in weaving together a grand story that ends in a wedding.

Many in the Church are embracing at least a basic level of the prophetic ministry that encourages, comforts, and builds up the Body of Christ. However, there is a deep longing to go deeper, desiring the anointing of the Spirit like Elijah had. However, Malachi said,

Remember the law of my servant Moses, the decrees and laws I gave him at Horeb for all Israel. See, I will send you the prophet Elijah before that great and dreadful day of the LORD comes. He will turn the hearts of the fathers to their children, and the hearts of the children to their fathers; or else I will come and strike the land with a curse. (Malachi 4:4-6)

Often, the most prophetic things we can possibly do is to turn our hearts to the next generation- understand the heart cry of the young ones.

This passage calls us to remember the "main and plain" things of scripture such as the death, burial and resurrection of Jesus, aiming for a Sermon on the Mount Lifestyle, loving others because we love Him, and attempting to love people into the kingdom. The Bible is clear on a number of different moral issues with multiple passages denouncing things such as idolatry, sorcery, sexual immorality, murder, and theft.

However, the passage also calls us to dump everything else for the sake of embracing others with the Gospel of the Kingdom. All of our "Isaacs" need to be put on the altar. Let's face it: If Jesus is desirable (As the Desire of the Nations) what in the relationship with our loved ones prevents them from seeing Jesus and wanting Him? This is a dangerous question to ask God because He will answer honestly and bluntly. Keep in mind that demons also know about this. They've inspired a pattern of relating in certain situations that prevents our loved ones from coming to Jesus. Paul laid everything he could down for the sake of turning people to Jesus.

It may mean sacrificing some of our "sacred cows" that are built *upon our interpretations of scripture*. Many traditions, "family values", norms, and values are not commanded in scripture. It is here the enemy will often whisper a lie related to fear that God will make known His displeasure for us for breaking with tradition. The Scripture is without flaw in its original autographs. We also have the Helper, the Spirit of Truth to give us understanding of scripture. However, our understanding and interpretation of scripture is often far from flawless because we still have areas that are not in perfect agreement with Jesus Christ.

For example, I have a beautiful sister that was also adopted from Korea. However, growing up, we had a bit of a sibling rivalry. As a teenager, I went after God the best I knew how as I was already experiencing some of the supernatural power of the Holy Spirit in prayer. Meanwhile, my sister went on to become an accomplished violist who played professionally for the orchestra-but she was not really going after Jesus in Jr. High.

One of the main things preventing my sister from turning to Jesus was *me*. There was a false sense of shame that if she came to Jesus after I did, it would prove that I am somehow better than her. However, when she became an accomplished violist and I honored her, her heart began to change. Eventually she went through the *Alpha* course and had a powerful encounter with Jesus. She also met a godly husband and they now have a beautiful family.

Fighting for the ones you love in intercession- removing the blinders:

However, we must also remember that our battle is in the supernatural, spiritual realm as well. There are supernatural barriers related to bringing our friends and family into the kingdom of God. The Apostle Paul gives us some understanding of these invisible (to the natural eye) spiritual obstacles:

And even if our gospel is veiled, it is veiled to those who are perishing. The god of this age has blinded the minds of unbelievers, so that they cannot see the light of the gospel of the glory of Christ, who is the image of God.
(2 Corinthians 4:3-4)

The reason why many of our friends, family, and other acquaintances do not love and follow Jesus is simply because *they cannot do so.* The enemy has supernaturally blinded their minds so that they cannot process truth at the heart-level and believe.

How does satan do this? Revelation 12 describes satan as the "accuser of the brethren". Satan and his demonic hordes launch accusations against us before the throne of God. According to Job 1 and 2 (and inferred by other scripture passages), satan still has access to God's justice system in the courts of heaven. He makes accusations against us on why God should not show mercy to us, but instead should bring his eternal wrath against us. However, the blood of Jesus still speaks a better word on our behalf including family, and friends.

Revelation 12 also describes a time when satan's appeals are exhausted and his access is cut off. He has a team of heavenly "lawyers" to oppose the overall purposes of God- including the gospel getting presented to every ethnic group. Thank God that we can understand the heart of the Judge presiding over this heavenly council.

However, satan doesn't only accuse us to God, he also accuses God to our loved ones. Unfortunately, he is quite effective at it- and he often uses the times where we have miss-represented Jesus- they got deeply wounded as the result. As we are made in the image of God, the potential to represent or miss-represent Jesus is greater than we can imagine. I've already highlighted about some of the practical, relational ways we can fight for the salvation of our loved ones and cut down the enemy's ability to use our sins and errors against us.

Using our own sins, their own brokenness, and negative events that he inspired, satan and his demonic forces exert a blinding influence upon the hearts of people. However, we can break this demonic "spell" so that people can hear the gospel. Paul prayed:

I keep asking that the God of our Lord Jesus Christ, the glorious Father may give you the Spirit of wisdom and revelation, so that you may know him better. I pray also that the eyes of your heart may be enlightened in order that you may know the hope to which he has called you, the riches of his glorious inheritance in the saints, and his incomparably great power for us who believe. (Ephesians 1:17-19)

Through the blood of Jesus- we have been given access to the throne of grace to make our petitions known on behalf of our loved ones.

One of the main ways to fight for family and friends is to pray for their salvation. We already know that God desires our family members to know Him-so we know we are praying according to God's will. God will not usurp anyone's ability to freely choose. However, we can ask God to remove the blinding influence of the demonic realm so that they can process truth at the heart-level and make an informed decision, unhindered by the demonic realm.

Often intercession for our loved ones in prayer makes the difference between life and death. In the midst of sharing the gospel on evangelism outreaches, I have found that virtually every single time someone gave their life to Jesus, they had someone faithfully praying for them to know Jesus. It does not guarantee that they will turn their lives over to Jesus, but usually over time, they will. God will give them opportunity after opportunity to process the truth without demonic interference. Persevering prayer is faith-filled prayer.

For example, I had been praying for my cousins on and off for years- that they would turn their lives completely over to Jesus. One of my cousins came out of a really messy situation family-wise. God had given my dad's side of the family has tremendous spiritual blessings- there are a number of powerful prayer warriors on that side of the family.

However, it is also pretty obvious that the enemy had done destructive things as well. I had lost track of what she was doing until I went to my Grandma's funeral. At the funeral, I found out that she was now married. Best of all, her and the whole family love Jesus and she was rather excited to talk to me about how Jesus had changed things in her life.

In another example, a different cousin ended up in jail after living quite wildly for a few years. It seemed like things were going from bad to worse for them. However, in the midst of heart-ache, Jesus Christ met him in a powerful way in answer to my prayer and the prayers of many others. After a season of discipleship and healing, my cousin is now an evangelist who leads hundreds of people to the Jesus every year. I am still fighting that my entire extended family would turn to Jesus through the removal of demonic blinding influences.

Another way that we can pray for our lost loved ones is to ask God to raise up anointed messengers. Jesus gave us insight into how he sees the people:

When he saw the crowds, he had compassion on them, because they were harassed and helpless, like sheep without a shepherd. Then he said to his disciples, "The harvest is plentiful but the workers are few. Ask the Lord of the harvest, therefore, to send out workers into his harvest field." (Matthew 9:37-38)

The Gospel of the kingdom is a "show and tell" gospel. It takes the anointing of the Holy Spirit to break the power of demonic bondages, healing the sick, and even raise the dead. Yet he is looking for people who are whole-hearted, wise, and trustworthy that God can anoint with this power.

Lord of the harvest, raise up laborers- but send someone else.
The problem is that the number of people that regularly practice loving other people towards and then into the kingdom is small. Evangelical studies indicate that less than 5% of believers in the United States ever lead someone else to Jesus. Paul said,

How then, can they call on the one they have not believed in? And how can they believe in the one of whom they have not heard? And how can they hear without someone preaching to them? And how can they preach unless they are sent? As it is written, "How beautiful are the feet of those who bring good news!" (Romans 10:14-15)

Meanwhile, we lament the dwindling influence of Biblical values in the culture and the lack of opportunities for our loved ones to be won to Jesus. Perhaps there is a correlation between these two problems.
Someone's last words are often some of their most important. Most of us know about Jesus' final commission to his disciples:

"All authority in heaven and on earth has been given to me. Therefore go and make disciples of all nations, baptizing them in the name of the Father and of the Son and of the Holy Spirit, and teaching them to obey everything I have commanded you. And surely, I am with you always, to the very end of the age." (Matthew 28:18-20)

Yet most of us don't regularly share the good news of the Kingdom because of fear: fear of failure, fear of what other people will think of us, fear of rejection, fear of losing our personal comforts and pleasures, fear over persecuted, fear of not doing it right etc. We need the peace of God upon our hearts or else we end up spiritually imparting fear when we attempt to lead people to Jesus-and people don't want that.
Jesus came to seek out and save the lost. In praying for other messengers to arise to share the gospel with our friends and family, isn't it a bit hypocritical to ask God to raise up messengers if

we are not willing to speak up on behalf of Jesus? Perhaps God wants to use you to be the answer to a father or mother's prayer for their children. Then everyone involved gets to share in the joy of God's saving activity.

When we regularly combine our prayers with attempting to love people into the kingdom of God, God starts putting people in the path of our family members and friends to share the gospel with them:

Do not be deceived: God cannot be mocked. A man reaps what he sows. The one who sows to please his sinful nature, from that nature will reap destruction; the one who sows to please the Spirit, from the Spirit will reap eternal life. Let us not become weary in doing good, for at the proper time we will reap a harvest if we do not give up. (Galatians 6:7-9)

A lifestyle of persistently aiming for full obedience to Jesus out of love for God and his people combined with prayer, fasting, and evangelism is an irresistible combination. Since satan and the demons don't have the fruit of the Spirit, the enemy inevitably ends up backing off.

For example, a young man named Kenny came to an evangelism training program I was helping to lead. Virtually every day of the program, the focus would be on prayer, getting a solid teaching on evangelism, and then going out and practicing what they learned in the teaching. I ended up partnering with Kenny a number of times in doing personal evangelism and a few people turned their lives over Jesus as the result.

Once the program ended, Kenny and his wife continued to evangelize back in their home town. A few weeks after the program ended, I got a *face book* message that he had the great joy of leading a couple of his family members to Jesus. Kenny had sowed salvation into the hearts of needy people and God saw to it that he would reap what he had just sown.

Spiritual warfare is real- and affects the things that are most dear to us: our relationship with Jesus, and the relationship with our family and friends. Sadly, it seems as if satan and his demons get away with a lot of oppression and attack against us and the ones he loves. In opening our hearts to God and partnering with Him with things that are dear to His heart, we can then use His name and spiritual authority to push back the enemy and rescue our loved ones from the cords of eternal death.

PART V:

INSIGHTS FROM
THE PROPHET DANIEL

13
<u>OVERCOMING</u>
<u>THE SEDUCTION OF BABYLON</u>

In July 2009, I was in trouble spiritually. My times in prayer were more of an angry wrestling match with God than adoration and fellowship. I had a very dark prophetic dream symbolically warning me that I was in danger. At a ministry conference, Benny Hinn warned about intentionally vexing the Holy Spirit through rebellion causing a quick response of repentance.

At that time, I did not believe in the danger of "falling away" from the faith through persistent rebellion, and refusing to forgive. I believed in once someone was saved, they were saved forever. However, the Holy Spirit spoke clear as day related to the coming Holy Spirit conference that I normally attend on July 29th, 2009:

Remember the warning I gave in December 2008? (Note: Mike Bickle preached extensively on the Harlot Babylon and the great falling away at the Onething conference in 2008) It was a warning about falling away because of <u>getting uprooted,</u> due to the strong winds that are coming. <u>Watch even in Minneapolis- St. Paul as I will release very strong winds as a sign </u>of the winds of the Spirit and adversity that are coming.

I rather reluctantly recorded the prophecy and promptly set it aside, not telling anyone- There was a conference to enjoy. I had no idea of the implications of what God was saying.

On the last day of the Holy Spirit conference, Graeme Cooke was talking related to wisdom. Suddenly, a tornado heading towards our location disrupted the whole conference. In scrambling for relative safety, all 1,200+ people end up hiding in small classrooms and the choir area. By "some chance" I end in the same room as Paul Anderson, (the director of the conference) and Pastor Fred Thoni (the man who oversaw the prophetic ministry at the conference). I showed them my dated journal entry and gave them a copy of the prophecy. People later gasped in awe as the leadership read the prophecy to everyone present at the conference.

Ten days later, the Evangelical Lutheran Church in America was in the middle of their national assembly. This was the day that the Lutheran Church-wide assembly was voting on the Social Statement: "Human Sexuality: Gift and trust". The primary issue in the statement was to condone monogamous homosexual relationships under "disputable matters" presuming the scriptures are not clear.

The problem is that scripture clearly addresses the issue of homosexual immorality (along with heterosexual immorality, greed, complaining, deception, treachery, bitterness, disobedience to parents etc.) as sin. Some Old Testament scriptures that describe this as sin include Genesis 19, Leviticus 18:22, and 20:13. Some New Testament scriptures that describe this as sin include Romans 1:26-27 and 1 Corinthians 6:9-11.

In voting to adapt the this "Human Sexuality: Gift and Trust", the Lutheran Church was directly voting whether to change the teachings of the Bible and becoming a stumbling block to millions of people. John Piper, a well-known pastor in the Minneapolis area, blogged on August 19th what happened next:

I saw the fast-moving, misshapen, unusually-wide funnel over downtown Minneapolis from Seven Corners. I said to Kevin Dau, "That looks serious."
It was. Serious in more ways than one. A friend who drove down to see the damage wrote,
On a day when no severe weather was predicted or expected...a tornado forms, baffling the weather experts—most saying they've never seen anything like it. It happens right in the city. The city: Minneapolis.

The tornado happens on a Wednesday...during the Evangelical Lutheran Church of America's national convention in the Minneapolis Convention Center. The convention is using Central Lutheran across the street as its church. The church has set up tents around it's building for this purpose.
According to the ELCA's printed convention schedule, at 2 PM on Wednesday, August 19, the 5th session of the convention was to begin. The main item of the session: "Consideration: Proposed Social Statement on Human Sexuality." The issue is

whether practicing homosexuality is a behavior that should disqualify a person from the pastoral ministry.

The eyewitness of the damage continues:
> *This curious tornado touches down just south of downtown and follows 35W straight towards the city center. It crosses I94. It is now downtown.*

The time: 2PM.

The first buildings on the downtown side of I94 are the Minneapolis Convention Center and Central Lutheran. The tornado severely damages the convention center roof, shreds the tents, breaks off the steeple of Central Lutheran, splits what's left of the steeple in two...and then lifts.

Let me venture an interpretation of this Providence with some biblical warrant.
1. The unrepentant practice of homosexual behavior (like other sins) will exclude a person from the kingdom of God.
The unrighteous will not inherit the kingdom of God? Do not be deceived: neither the sexually immoral, nor idolaters, nor adulterers, nor men who practice homosexuality, nor thieves, nor the greedy, nor drunkards, nor revilers, nor swindlers will inherit the kingdom of God." (1 Corinthians 6:9-10)

2. The church has always embraced those who forsake sexual sin but who still struggle with homosexual desires, rejoicing with them that all our fallen, sinful, disordered lives (all of us, no exceptions) are forgiven if we turn to Christ in faith.
Such were some of you. But you were washed, you were sanctified, you were justified in the name of the Lord Jesus Christ and by the Spirit of our God. (1 Corinthians 6:11)

3. Therefore, official church pronouncements that condone the very sins that keep people out of the kingdom of God, are evil. They dishonor God, contradict Scripture, and implicitly promote damnation where salvation is freely offered.

4. Jesus Christ controls the wind, including all tornados.
Who then is this, that even the wind and the sea obey him? (Mark 4:41)

5. When asked about a seemingly random calamity near Jerusalem where 18 people were killed, Jesus answered in general terms—an

answer that would cover calamities in Minneapolis, Taiwan, or Baghdad. God's message is repent, because none of us will otherwise escape God's judgment.
Jesus: "Those eighteen on whom the tower in Siloam fell and killed them: do you think that they were worse offenders than all the others who lived in Jerusalem? No, I tell you; but unless you repent, you will all likewise perish." (Luke 13:4-5)

6. Conclusion: The tornado in Minneapolis was a gentle but firm warning to the ELCA and all of us: Turn from the approval of sin. Turn from the promotion of behaviors that lead to destruction. Reaffirm the great Lutheran heritage of allegiance to the truth and authority of Scripture. Turn back from distorting the grace of God into sensuality. Rejoice in the pardon of the cross of Christ and its power to transform left and right wing sinners[4].

Sadly, in spite of God putting his displeasure on display for all to see over this statement (see Jeremiah 23:19-20), the Evangelical Lutheran Church of America voted to affirm "Human Sexuality: Gift and trust". As another sign- the vote was exactly the 2/3rds majority needed (.666) out of over 1,000 votes cast.

Understanding the seduction of the Harlot Babylon

As we covered in chapters 2 and 3, God is at work to bring the heavens and the earth under the leadership of Jesus. Meanwhile, satan is also working (with the permission of Jesus) to bring a counterfeit convergence of the demonic kingdom and the material realm as well. The height of satan's wisdom will produce the Harlot of all Harlots:

Then the angel carried me away in the Spirit to the desert. There I saw a woman sitting on a scarlet beast that was covered with blasphemous names and had seven heads and ten horns. The woman was dressed in purple and scarlet, and was glittering with gold, precious stones and pearls. She held a golden cup in her hand, filled with abominable things and the fifth of her adulteries. The time was written on her forehead:

MYSTERY
BABYLON THE GREAT
THE MOTHER OF PROSTITUTES
AND OF THE ABOMINATIONS OF THE EARTH.

[4] www.desiringgod.org Copyright 2009 by John Piper, used by permission

I saw that the woman was drunk with the blood of the saints, the blood of those who bore testimony of Jesus. (Revelation 17:3-6)

In this passage of scripture, I will highlight six different ways that the height of "satan's wisdom" will attempt to seduce the saints into turning their backs on Jesus:

1. Confusion about "grace" that emboldens people to sin.
        In Genesis 11, the place was named "Babel" after God confused all the languages. In preparation, a whole generation has been emboldened to sin without limit through listening to false teachers and false prophets. Scripture warns numerous times of false teachers within the Body of Christ that will deceive many into a lifestyle of compromise with sin. The current assault against the doctrine of grace is satan's preparation for this harlot Babylon to arise. The sin will eventually grow into full-blown rebellion against Jesus even to the point of permanently renouncing faith in Jesus.

2. The Seduction of occult supernatural power:
        Babylon literally means "gate of the gods". In Genesis 11, the people built the tower of Babel to bring about their own false convergence between the supernatural realm (demons) and the physical material realm apart from Jesus. Scripture compares idol worship and sorcery to harlotry- it breaks God's heart. All of the religious systems on earth (except Jesus-centered biblical Christianity that promotes the wisdom of God) will be combined and accepted as a way to show demonstrations of demonic power to suppress the truth. Satan will offer the "best of the best" displays of evil supernatural power through sorcery under the Babylonian religious, system- even to the point of calling fire down from heaven.

3. Seduction of immorality and sensuality
        We've already mentioned the issue of sexual immorality and other sensual pleasures (drugs, alcohol etc.) as a "false comforts". However the depths of sexual immorality and perversion will touch the earth like never before. The depths of sexual perversion will lead to un-paralleled oppression of the weak and the broken for self-centered gratification. We can already see the edges of this through the epidemic of human trafficking and internet pornography.

134

4. Seduction of wealth and materialism

Scripture warns that the love of money is the root of all evil. The Harlot Babylon will seduce people through offering "bragging rights" (the one who has the most toys wins), and every convenience and comfort that wealth can buy. Money can also buy influence as recent U.S. presidential elections attest to. The Harlot Babylon economic system will bring a false security and peace to those ensnared by it. The wealth will be intermingled with political and religious power to seduce many into compromise and then rebellion.

5. Seduction of control and political power

The Babylonian system will be the largest and most prestigious social and relational network in history spanning across all cultural boundaries. God confused the speech and interaction of the nations in Genesis 11 to slow down the progress of destructive, self-centered evil. It will be the ultimate humanistic self-centered spiritual, political, economic, and sensual pleasure network in history.

6. The threat of loss, suffering, and death (persecution).

To those who refuse to enter into the pleasures offered by the Babylonian system (the heights of the wisdom of satan), and denounce it, there is a down-side. The Harlot Babylon system will publicly humiliate, torture, and kill many who oppose it. The physical agony of those who reject this "Mystery Babylon" will bring perverted pleasure to evil people as bitterness and rage will have a legal expression.

The Harlot Babylon will combine these six dimensions of sowing sin to produce temporary self-centered ecstasy. It will be the height of satan's case that his false wisdom (from James chapter 3) can produce the superior pleasures over God's wisdom in the human experience. However, this temporary human system then reaps the eternal bitter harvest of God's judgment.

How can the saints withstand her seduction?

God's wisdom and power will not outdone by the wisdom of Satan at the end of the age. Jesus is the still the author of superior pleasure from eternity past (Psalm 16). The first commandment will have first place in the Church. The joy of unstoppable, unquenchable love in God overflowing to other people will trump every other pleasure:

Let him kiss me with the kisses of his mouth-for your love is more delightful than life. *(Song of Songs 1:2)*

Simply abiding in the Word of God is sufficient. Do we realize what God, the author of pleasure, is offering us forever? God's pleasures are so overwhelming that we will need new physical, resurrected bodies to be able fully experience them. At the end of this age, God will pour out abundant grace by the power of the Spirit to overcome satan's wisdom with the superior pleasures of God. To illustrate, let's compare the life of Solomon to the life of Paul.

Solomon had everything anyone could have wanted in this world. He lived in the finest house, drank the choicest of wines, ate the finest of foods every day, He wore the finest of clothes. When he traveled, he traveled in luxurious escort. Solomon had the finest of service and entertainment at his finger tips.

Solomon ruled the most powerful nation during a time of peace. No one else dared challenge Israel militarily. As the son of King David, he enjoyed the honor of the throne of Israel. His words were law. No one within the kingdom questioned his wisdom or judgment. He had no political enemies domestically. The men of Israel willingly struck down insurrectionists before they could even get started. The heads of nations came and paid him respect, finances, and luxuries to gain some knowledge and wisdom.

In a religious sense, he had everything. He had the promise that his kingdom would go forever as he inherited the promises given to David. He had the finest scribes and priests available to declare the law to him. Solomon undertook the grandest project of all-the building of the temple. He built the temple with the finest materials. God then validated his work with fire from heaven. Solomon wrote his place in eternity. He wrote much of the Book of Proverbs. With incredible depth of insight, he wrote the Song of Songs-illustrating the growth and maturing of love: God to humanity along with husband and wife.

Unfortunately, Solomon's wisdom did not keep growing as did his great knowledge. Unfortunately, Solomon took in great wealth along with the foreign wives which God had forbidden of the king in Deuteronomy 17:16-17. Solomon departed from God's ways of humility and eventually it led him into idolatry.

Near the end of His life, Solomon still possessed great knowledge and wisdom. Yet, the fiery passion and joy over God was gone. He had acted foolishly in seeking after other gods. His heart had grown cold and bitter towards God after discipline was pronounced against his descendents. Solomon had become like Saul in that he tried to kill Jeroboam (1 Kings 11:26-40). At the end of his life, Solomon records his depression and despair.

The words of the Teacher, son of David, king in Jerusalem:

"Meaningless! Meaningless!"
says the Teacher.
"Utterly meaningless!
Everything is meaningless." (Ecclesiastes 1:1-2.)

Meanwhile, contrast the life of Solomon to the life of the Apostle Paul. The Apostle Paul had no earthly luxuries. Most of the time, he only traveled with the clothes on his back. Paul often went without food-sometimes for periods of up to 40 days and nights. He was shipwrecked several times. He spent a number of years in prison chained in place with rats and flies circling about. There was never any certainty of seeing another day.

He spent his life on the run as a fugitive of his own countrymen. Always in danger he fled in secret, hiding in caves and other out of the way places. Once caught, he was stoned at least one time, beaten with rods, endured the 40 minus one lash scourging several times for "heresy", and left for dead at least once. He didn't build a monument for himself. He did no earthly great things-except causing several disturbances and riots.

Paul faced enemies from within and without. A number of his own brethren usurped his honor in the Corinthian church. Those who were supposed to be on his side criticized him for preaching to the Gentiles. Others demanded him to be killed. Then there was the state of Rome that helped him at times and hindered him at others.

In all of his trials and troubles, he had one thing at the end of his life. The opportunities for release or more fruitful service were gone. Many of the people within the churches had risen up and led the followers of Christ astray. Imprisoned without any earthly hope, execution loomed. Most of his closet followers had deserted him out of fear. Yet he writes to Timothy:

I have fought the good fight, I have finished the race, I have kept the faith. Now there is in store for me the crown of righteousness, which the Lord, the righteous Judge, will award to me on that day-and not only to me, but also to all who have longed for his appearing. (2 Timothy 4:7-8)

Hardly last words of despair, these are last words of triumph! Both of Solomon and Paul experienced supernatural revelation at the highest levels. Yet they had two different reviews upon their lives. What made the difference?

The example of Daniel in the midst of seduction and great hardship:

It was in the early 600's BC and Josiah was reigning on the throne. The whole nation is apparently in a flood-tide of renewal and revival as Josiah had just renewed the nation's covenant with the God of Abraham, Isaac, and Jacob. The Asherah pole (a center of demonic worship) is torn down. Other centers of idolatry and abominable practices are desecrated and shut down. There is excitement and relative prosperity in the land- God is still for us with prosperity and prominence are apparently just around the corner. There is an assumption that prophetic promises related to the temple of the LORD from hundreds of years ago will protect the people. In the midst of this, Daniel grew up as a teen-ager in the royal family. We find Daniel "on fire for God" in the midst of much idolatry and corruption.

Suddenly everything has changed: Ominous clouds of judgment now loom over the land. With the new king, the historic practices of idolatry are once again the "in thing" to do in the land. Captivity is coming because of the harlotry of Judah, particularly due to the corruption of its leaders (the priests and the prophets).

In another dramatic turn of events, without warning Babylon invades Judah and now Daniel and his family are taken captive to Babylon where more trouble waited: Undoubtedly Daniel saw some of his family get killed by the Babylonians. He was in an unfamiliar land with unfamiliar language and customs.

Worst of all, Daniel was undoubtedly "eunuched" (Isaiah 39:7; 2 Kings 20:16-18) at the hands of the King of Babylon. First this meant that Daniel would never be able to have offspring. Biblically, this is usually presented as a great judgment for abominable sin (2 Samuel 6:23; 1 Kings 14:10; 21:20-22). Second, even if circumstances changed, Daniel would never again be able to enter into the assembly at the temple (Deuteronomy 23:1).

So on the surface, in response to being "on fire for God" as a youth, the answer appears to be a life-time ban from entering God's temple, humiliation, barrenness, grief, and other types of suffering associated with being captive in Babylon. In the midst of this suffering there was a seductive offer through the Babylonian culture: *"Forget about the pain of the past dealings with God and drown it out with the finest food, wine, and luxury from Babylon- where was God when all this other negative stuff was happening to you?"* In the midst of the seduction and persecution, Daniel's love did not grow cold.

What did Daniel Know about God?

From Daniel 9, we can clearly understand that Daniel was paying attention to the prophesying of Jeremiah and Isaiah. Jeremiah had prophesied about Babylon's invasion and Israel's captivity from God (Jeremiah 25:8-11). Meanwhile, Isaiah spoke of a king named Cyrus who would let the people go back to the land (Isaiah 44:26-45:3).

Since the scrolls of Isaiah and Jeremiah did not have chapter and verses, we know Daniel was looking absorbing their whole messages. Therefore, Daniel knew that all the negative things happening to him were not because God was personally angry with him. Daniel understood that God was judging the whole nation for its corporate culture of idolatry and oppression. The root cause of Daniel's misery was the idolatrous practices of the nation and he identified it as the culprit in Daniel 9:7-10 for which God would be required to pour out his judgments.

In the midst of the shame, humiliation, despair, and hopelessness of the captivity situation in Babylon, Daniel surely found God's unique promise to those who would otherwise be disqualified under the law (mainly those who were now "eunuched" or foreigners):

Let no foreigner who has bound himself to the LORD say, "The LORD will surely exclude me from his people." And let not any eunuch complain, "I am only a dry tree". For this is what the LORD says: "To the eunuchs who keep my Sabbaths, who choose what pleases me and hold fast to my covenant- to them I will give within my temple and its walls a memorial and name better than sons and daughters; I will give them an everlasting name that will not be cut off." (Isaiah 56:3-5)

Since God had fulfilled the negative part of the words of Isaiah and Jeremiah, He believed the positive parts as well. Daniel took this prophetic promise and he made it his own.

We find later in his life in Daniel 9 that God indeed took his prayers as a youth very seriously. Daniel dared to believe His Word through Isaiah to find himself in the story-and demonstrated his faith with his counter-cultural lifestyle. In response, God sent high-level angelic messengers to confirm Daniel's identity in the story calling him "highly esteemed"- Jesus would later reference this man in the midst of His ministry.

14

OVERCOMING THE BITTER ENVY OF PERSIA

In September 2002, my home local Church BPLC was hosting a special healing service where we would wait upon the Holy Spirit to move in power among us. I was chosen by the staff of BPLC to be the prayer captain than night. I now know that this could have stirred up some "funny feelings" among some of God's favorite intercessors in the church who were older and wiser.

A few years earlier, I had been praying with some older ladies in a prayer group. These dear women of God stood in the gap and kept BPLC afloat during very lean times with their heart-felt cries before Jesus. Suddenly, new leadership came in 1996 and they felt marginalized as God raised up others who also had powerful prayer lives. As I was slowly maturing in prayer they suddenly let me know they didn't want me in their prayer group. Now I was going to be leading them again.

Not understanding much about relational dynamics at the time, I decided I would do a holy "science experiment". I would go on a one day fast and ask God to anoint the other intercessors far more than anything I experienced. I would suffer some hunger pains so that others could have great joy in operating under a greater measure of the anointing of the Holy Spirit.

To my great delight, God answered in prayer that night beyond anything I could have imagine. The rest of the prayer ministry team came back with reports of physical healing and emotional healing in answer to their prayers. Some said it was the best time of prayer ministry they had ever had. The service went for hours as people enjoyed the refreshing presence of Jesus.

Of course, God then turned around and blessed me in incredible ways as well. The worship leader had been to the IHOP-KC harp and bowl conference and got the idea to add a prayer leader to the worship team. That evening in September 2002 marked the beginning of an 11-month journey with many difficulties and trials that would bring me into full-time intercessory prayer ministry at IHOP-KC in 2003.

Lessons from Daniel: A confrontation with bitter envy

In Daniel 6, we find that something unusual had just happened: Persia had just replaced Babylon as the dominating power. Daniel who had been cut out of the scene for a number of years under King Belshazzar of Babylon was now suddenly in a major leadership role. Scripture tells us:

It pleased Darius to appoint 120 satraps to rule throughout the kingdom, with three administrators over them, one of whom was Daniel. The satraps were made accountable to them so that the king might not suffer loss. Now Daniel so distinguished himself among the administrators and the satraps by his exceptional qualities that the king planned to set him over the whole kingdom. (Daniel 6:1-3)

In the last chapter on Babylon, we find that Daniel had made a deep commitment to God to resist the spirit behind the Babylonian culture. Daniel had been promoted and then demoted under Babylonian rule. Suddenly Daniel was promoted again into primary leadership-and was in line for greater promotion: The king wanted to put him in charge over the whole kingdom like Joseph in Egypt.

However, if Daniel is put into a primary leadership position, it means that others are not. Other leaders were gripped with bitter envy. Perhaps they had served the king faithfully for decades. How could this "hot shot" foreigner that formerly served Persia's enemy possibly be promoted above them! Scripture tells us:

At this, the administrators and satraps tried to find grounds for charges against Daniel in his conduct of government affairs, but they were unable to do so. They could find no corruption in him because he was trustworthy and neither corrupt or negligent. Finally, these men said, "We will never find basis for charges against this man Daniel unless it has something to do with the law of his God." (Daniel 6:4-5)

As the rest of the story unfolds, they end up manipulating the king into attempting to execute Daniel. God sent the angel to shut the mouths of the lions and Daniel was vindicated.

Behind the scenes related to this drama was that Daniel was praying in Daniel 9 and 10. In the third year of Cyrus, King of

Persia, Daniel had a vision (Daniel 10:1) and then God sent a mighty angel with the specific interpretation in Daniel 10:

Then he (the angel) ***continued, "Do not be afraid, Daniel. Since the first day that you set your mind to gain understanding and to humble yourself before your God, your words were heard, and I have come in response to them. But the prince of the Persian Kingdom resisted me twenty-one days. Then Michael, one of the chief princes, came to help me, because I was detained there with the king of Persia. (Daniel 10:12-13)***

In answer to Daniel's intercession to God related to the release of Israel from captivity, God sent the angel. A demon called "the prince of the Persian Kingdom" stopped him. At the same time, the Prince of Persia was stirring up bitter envy in the hearts of these other governmental leaders against Daniel in Daniel 6. God then sent Michael the arch-angel to push back this demonic king. We all know the rest of the story- Israel was released from captivity to return to rebuild the temple and Jerusalem to prepare for the first coming of Jesus.

Perhaps there is no greater threat to the purposes of God than bitter envy leading to hatred and a spirit of murder. Some theologians believe that it was because of bitter envy over the coming creation of human beings that satan rebelled against God bringing division in heaven.

We see the killer threat of bitter envy throughout Biblical history. In the first family, satan stirred up the bitter envy in Cain's heart after God honored Abel's offering (and apparently choosing his family line as the chosen seed to crush satan) while ignoring Cain's offering. Cain did not resist it with the grace of God and it grew into hatred and Cain killed of Abel. Abraham had to send Hagar and Ishmael away who was taunting and mistreating Isaac. The result has been a deep wound in the hearts of many people in the Middle East. Satan has historically taken advantage of this to stir up hatred towards the Jewish people and the Middle East is a boiling pot of tension waiting to explode.

Esau was filled with bitter envy and hatred for Jacob- until he saw what it meant to be chosen and what Jacob had endured to become that chosen vessel. King Saul was filled with bitter envy and attempted to kill David in a rage. Over and over again, we can see how satan tried to take out God's anointed through bitter envy leading to murder.

Even on a local level, bitter envy is a key tactic of the enemy that leads to division and broken relationships. Bitter envy towards people that God gives a season of unusual favor is often responsible for poisoning relational soul-ties. From chapter 10 we understand that "prayers" released out of these poisoned soul ties can harm people emotionally and physically. Many kingdom initiatives within local churches have been aborted because of bitter envy of the ones that God chose to anoint.

Why does God choose to exalt people?

Jesus gave us the parable of the talents in Matthew 25:14-30. Like the master in the parable, God deliberately gives some people more talents than other people. Paul wrote that Holy Spirit distributes gifts according to His will. Simply observing people shows that God has given some people more than others in the area of physical ability, emotional and relational abilities, intellectual giftedness, supernatural abilities that are dependent on the Spirit, and economic resources.

God has all the power and authority and He does with it what He pleases. Scripture also tells us that God establishes those who have authority. Scripture warns:

Do not lift your horns against heaven; do not speak with outstretched neck. No one from the east or the west or from the desert can exalt a man. But it is God who judges; He brings one down, he exalts another. (Psalm 75:5-7)

In other words, God deliberately gives some more than others. God deliberately exalts some people over others. Why?

First, we need to look at some enemy deceptions that need to be corrected or if God "chooses" us for a special role, these deceptions will hatch and cause selfish conceit that leads to destruction.

God does not exalt people because God loves one person over another person. The expression of God's love towards each of us needs to be measured by what Jesus did at the cross for us- not at the amount of temporary favor or power God has given me compared to you. Luke 15 tells us that God would have done it even if you were the only one who was lost. God has made us unique and beloved in Jesus. Just because God exalts you over me in a leadership role doesn't mean that God likes you more than me. On the other hand if God exalt me over you in spiritual anointing to heal the sick, it doesn't mean that God loves me more than you.

God does not exalt people to prominence or leadership because the person was dedicated or because they "earned" it. God esteems our love and our dedication to Him by His grace. However, there is no possible way that we can earn God's favor with people and God's power to make wealth or supernatural power to heal cancer. Whatever good we have, it is because of the grace and the mercy of God.

God does not exalt people to prominence or leadership for the sake of the individual receiving benefits. Often the exact opposite is true. Often those that God exalts come under greater spiritual attack of the devil, more difficulty, more pain, and more pressure from people. Favor and crowds are fickle- they can be really glad one day and really mad the next. However, what is guaranteed is that to whom much is given, much is required.

So why does God exalt and anoint individuals with unusual measures of favor and blessing upon their lives. It's not directly a spiritual merit badge. It's not for the personal benefits of the one who gets exalted and it's not because God loves you more than the next guy.

First, God exalts people to fulfill his promised prophetic words and overall redemptive plan. In scripture, we find that God raised up some unusual people: God raised up a gentile king named Cyrus to set the Jewish people free, even proclaiming his destiny before he was born.

Surprisingly in many cases, God allows satan to exalt someone who is deeply rebellious to his plan and purposes who then unwittingly does God's plan anyway. For example, God raised up pharaoh of Egypt who was deeply opposed to letting the Jewish people go so that Israel would see God's glory and mighty power in action in the book of Exodus. God raised up Assyria and Babylon to chastise Israel for their idolatry. At the very end, God will allow satan to raise up the anti-christ, a world dictator that is the most evil man that has ever lived on the earth. However, once God is done with the rebellious, He judges them and punishes them forever.

Second, God sometimes chooses people and exalts people to force everyone to choose humility by exposing pride. Beginning with the choice of the Jewish people from the loins of Abraham, God said to Israel:

The LORD did not set his affection on you and choose you because you were more numerous than other peoples, for you were the fewest of all peoples. (Deuteronomy 7:7)

God chose the weakest to lead history forward unto global salvation. In doing so, every nation had to choose whether to humble themselves to this tiny people group or boast in the strength of their might. Paul wrote of this dynamic to the Corinthian believers:

145

But God chose the foolish things of the world to shame the wise; God chose the weak things of the world to shame the strong. He chose the lowly things of this world and the despised things- and things that are not to nullify the things that are, so that no one may boast before him.
(1 Corinthians 1:27-29)

At times, God will use deliberately use people everyone else "writes off" in dramatic and powerful ways simply to offend the proud. Remember, God deliberately exposes dangerous amounts of arrogant pride with either bitter envy or a bitter entitlement mentality that comes out when people or God offend us.

Third, God chooses people for exalted leadership positions and blesses them for the sake of making them a blessing to others. We see this as well in God choosing the Jewish people as his priestly people to lead the way unto global redemption. Paul wrote that Jesus gives *people* as gifts to the Body of Christ:

It was he who gave some to be apostles, some to be prophets, some to be evangelists, and some to be pastors and teachers, to prepare God's people for works of service so that the body of Christ may be built up until we all reach unity in the faith and in the knowledge of the Son of God and become mature, attaining to the whole measure of the fullness of Christ. (Ephesians 4:11-13)

God deliberately "exalts" people by giving an unusual measure of grace in some areas to challenge the whole Body of Christ to grow in that area. How the Church receives them determines the measure of breakthrough in the area of need.

The principle is first found in Genesis 12:1-3 where God chose Abram to be blessed to be a blessing to every ethnic group on the earth. God gave Joseph unusual favor for the sake of bringing provision for the entire earth. After all of the difficulties that David went through, the scriptures say:

And David knew that the LORD had established him as king over Israel and had exalted his kingdom for the sake of his people Israel. (2 Samuel 5:12)

David had been given prophetic promises in the wilderness as a youth (Psalm 132:1-4) that were confirmed by Samuel. Now decades later, they were coming to pass by the sovereign God for the sake of His redemptive purposes.

In one sense, we cannot earn God's grace or favor with our diligence in prayer. However, through diligence, we can position ourselves before God and other people so that God can pour greater grace upon us to be used by God for the sake of others. Spiritual disciplines such as practicing the Sermon on the Mount Lifestyle, fasting, prayer, extravagant giving, walking in humility when it hurts etc. prepare us to be that great blessing to other people that Jesus would receive greater glory on the earth in this age.

God's glory cloaked in the midst of brokenness.

God hates conceit and pride with passion- it ruined paradise and divided heaven producing untold measures of pain and suffering. He also understands that it is deeply imbedded in the human heart. Scripture and human history show that wealth, supernatural power, and unusual knowledge cause people to become "puffed up" with pride- that leads to their destruction.

Meanwhile, God also loves his beloved ones with a jealous passion as His treasured ones. He wants to overwhelm his beloved ones with his goodness. This presents a dilemma: How can God release great blessing to His beloved ones, when such blessings tend to produce conceit in the hearts of mankind which God hates with a passion?

Of course, God had the answer before there was a problem: *To prevent destructive pride, God allows His beloved ones to get crushed before He exalts them in extreme ways.* In Biblical and Church history, the way God deals with human pride is that He kills it. He allows a crushing of the ones He wants to use in an overwhelming way to bless others. God's goal is that He would find people void of conceit. Often, God will allow the bitter envy and hatred of others stirred up by satan to do the job for Him. Joseph was sold into slavery and then put in prison. In the midst of the prison sentences, Joseph learned how to be a father, not simply a favored brother. God sent Moses into the wilderness for 40 years of "meaningless activity" except for his communion to God.

Even in the midst of God using someone in incredible ways, God will deliberately allow hardship, internal difficulty, and mistreatment of His favorite ones to prevent conceit from developing. Writing of an internal problem, (in contrast to the external persecution and difficulty previously), Paul wrote:

To keep me from becoming conceited because of these surpassingly great revelations, there was given me a thorn in my flesh, a messenger of Satan, to torment me. Three times I pleaded with the Lord to take it away from me. But he said to me, "My grace is sufficient for you, for my power is made perfect in weakness." Therefore I will boast all the more gladly about my weaknesses, so that Christ's power may rest on me. (2 Corinthians 12:7-9)

In other words, God deliberately cloaks the greatest manifestations of his power and glory in the midst of weakness because He is Jealous to protect their heart.

God's Holy Jealousy over the hearts of His beloved ones

God first revealed himself as a Jealous God at the foot of Mount Sinai in the book of Exodus. The people trembled as the presence and power of God shook the whole mountain. Fire and smoke covered the top with lightning bolts flashing from the Presence of God. In the midst of this heavenly betrothal time God said,

I, the LORD your God, am a jealous God... (Exodus 20:4)

God is claiming rightful possession of His people, but God's Holy Jealousy is completely different from bitter envy.

Most of us are familiar with bitter envy- and our willingness to kill to get certain things for our own selfish pleasures. God's Holy Jealousy is completely the opposite:

Let us fix our eyes on Jesus, the author and perfecter of our faith, who for the joy set before him endured the cross, scorning its shame, and sat down at the right hand of the throne of God. (Hebrews 12:2)

Jesus shared why He was doing this with his first disciples before he would go to the cross:

"I tell you, I will not drink of this fruit of the vine from now until that day when I drink it anew with you in my Father's kingdom."(Matthew 26:29)

The joy in Jesus' heart was for you to one day experience the fullness of joy and pleasure found at the Father's right hand. Instead of killing for selfish purpose and pleasure, Jesus would rather lay down his life for us, than to see us miss out and get the full trouble our sin deserved. Even now, Jesus is our Great High Priest who lives to make intercession for us.

This is the God who has all the wisdom, all the power, all the resources, and all the knowledge to do anything He wants- *without violating anyone's ability to choose.* Meanwhile, God is for us with a Holy Jealousy both individually, and the corporate Body of Christ. This is the God who is leading history- we have an unbelievably secure and glorious future.

Consequently, when I choose to do my own thing (satan's wisdom) instead of following God's ways, I deeply break his heart. To the ones who deeply choose Him, God will often give them a small taste of the grief and pain in His heart when love is scorned for selfishness like in the "dark night of faith" in Song of Songs 5. God is looking for a heart cry to come forth in the midst of the confusion and pain: *"Jesus, I NEVER want you to feel that pain of scorned love from me again because I love you so much."*

God is jealous for you and me to experience His best joy and pleasure forever. Meanwhile, the same God has all the knowledge, wisdom, and power to lead our lives perfectly without violating anyone's free will. In other words, our future joy and glory is secure in following His leadership by grace. We've got it made!

Holy Jealousy- a key to the floods of revival?

What if our identity was so secure in the reality of God's Holy Jealousy over us that we can then stop fighting for our own places and future and turn to fight on behalf of the other brothers and sisters in Christ? What happens if this same "Holy Jealousy of God" gets deeply in our own hearts? Jesus prayed in John 17

I have made you known to them, and will continue to make you known in order that <u>the love you have for me may be in them</u> and that I myself may be in them. (John 17:26)

Jesus had just prayed that we would be one with God as God is with God…and one with each other and see the glory of God in John 17:20-25. Perhaps this understanding of the Holy Jealous love from God is the key.

In church history, when revival starts there is great excitement. However the human dynamics of some leaders getting exalted (with accompanying wealth, honor, and further opportunities) above others usually stirs up both self-centered conceit (among those "chosen" for long-term special roles), and bitter envy (among those not chosen). They are both signs that dangerous amounts of conceit and human pride are present- the wisdom of satan. Often the feelings in the heart lead to actions such as manipulation, gossip, slander, or other more obvious forms of sin.

As the result, satan often ends up succeeding in bringing division and strife among the leaders which eventually choke off the move of the Holy Spirit. The focus gets distracted related to the money, honor, and opportunities. Since it is no longer centered on Jesus, God slowly withdraws His manifest presence until the next time He can find a place to pour out His Spirit again.

In the midst of this, God cried out through the prophet Isaiah to Israel and the Body of Christ world-wide:

Heaven is my throne, and the earth is my footstool. Where is t he house you will build for me? Where will my resting place be? (Isaiah 66:1)

Each time the Holy Spirit has been poured out through history, God has been emphasizing key truth of scripture in the midst of a massive building project. However, God is looking for a temple made of living stones with flesh where God's glory can once again rest upon like when His glory came down and rested upon Mount Sinai.

One of the hidden heroes of the faith was Pat Bickle, who lived rather different circumstances than his famous brother, Mike. In high school, Pat Bickle was injured in a football accident and paralyzed from the neck down. His story was covered by the KC Star.

Pat's mind was sharp, but physically, he could virtually do nothing. Confined to a hospital bed, he would live this way for 30+ years. While Mike was famous, traveling, and preaching to thousands of people and leading Kansas City Fellowship- Pat was on his back, only occasionally counseling a young man or woman to love Jesus at his bed- while waiting to be raised up by God.

In 2007, IHOP-KC and GOD-TV were joining forces and Mike Bickle was beginning to enter into some of his prophetic promises. Wealth, honor, popularity, power, new opportunity, and excitement filled IHOP-KC- especially Mike. Meanwhile, Pat Bickle became extremely ill with pneumonia and other health problems. Instead of God raising him up, things were getting worse physically! What about God's promises? Is God really faithful to His word?

With every earthly reason and opportunity for self-pity and bitter-envy, Pat resisted this and continued to love Jesus to the very end. Only someone touched by the Holy Jealousy of God and absolutely convinced of the worthiness of Jesus to receive His reward could finish this way. Jesus finally came on May 5th, 2007 and took Pat Bickle home to be with Him-without physically raising him up.

Someone who overcame bitter envy/ self-centeredness at such an extraordinary level to continue to love Jesus whole-heartedly to the very end qualifies for the Hebrews 11 hall of faith.

While we don't yet fully understand the significance, Pat Bickle broke through against bitter envy in an extraordinary way. Due to Pat's courage, church history is closer to the moment that revival will start- and never end.

15

OVERCOMING THE CRUSHING DISAPPOINTMENT FROM GREECE

In chapter 3, we looked at God's overall redemptive plan: The Father is bringing heaven and earth under the leadership of Jesus and it has vast implications. We also looked at the Greek worldview and its negative implications along with the Hebraic worldview.

Scripture indicates that behind the Greek mindset is a huge demonic "prince". The angel gave the prophet Daniel this message:

So he said, "Do you know why I have come to you? Soon I will return to fight against the prince of Persia, and when I go, the prince of Greece will come; but first I will tell you what is written in the Book of Truth. (No one supports me against them except Michael, your prince.)(Daniel 10:20-21)

If we look at the whole of Daniel 7-12, we can find that there is an emphasis on the empire of Greece. Paul the apostle attempted to preach the Gospel with power in Athens, Greece in Acts 17. However, only some of the people believed and no notable miracles were reported. Paul left Greece disappointed and discouraged.

The demonic stinger behind practical humanism: Hope deferred

If anyone closely follows Jesus for any length of time, invariably there are times when God's activity makes no sense. *Why didn't God answer our prayer for healing when_____ died? Why did God not come through in_____? God spoke prophetically and confirmed it in dramatic fashion!* I've personally been stung by this insidious tactic of the enemy.

In May of 2001, I was riding high on Monday morning and excited as I went in to the office to serve at a city-wide prayer ministry in the Twin Cities. God had done great things and I was expecting that my ministry with this city-wide prayer ministry would continue and grow- I would serve them and continue with my part-time job at ACR homes over the summer.

Previously, in late August of 2000, I was looking for an internship as part of my graduation requirements for seminary. I was serving my local church in the prayer ministry. However, I got a letter from *Pray Minnesota* and Pastor Steve Loopstra. After I had attended in 1999 as a delegate, they were looking for people to serve on the steering committee. I got in contact with the leadership of *Pray Minnesota!* I was interested in serving and learning from them. I arranged a meeting with Pastor Steve.

The day of the meeting, I went out to start my truck and my truck would not start. In a panic, I called my parents to see if I could get some help. Meanwhile, I kept hearing a voice, *"Go out and command the thing to start in the name of Jesus"*. Finally, I went out, turned the key after commanding my truck to start in Jesus' name and suddenly I was driving to downtown Minneapolis. The meeting was pivotal and I joined in their ministry team.

Suddenly, I was given access to city-wide events as a leader. I learned how the various parts of seeking transformation could work together: The pastors needed to be in unity by the grace of God, the intercessors needed to be in place, key business and civic leaders need to be part of the leadership team as well. In a city-wide event called *Arise with the Guys* dozens of people gave their lives to Jesus for the first-time and hundreds rededicated their lives back to Jesus.

That morning, I was brought in and the leadership of the ministry informed me that they had prayed about whether I was to continue and they did not feel the grace of God on it. In other words, today was going to be the last day. *What?!?*

Confused, disappointed, and angry at God, I went home feeling as if I did not have a future. How could God say "No" without telling me about it first?

Without clear answers from God, typically hope deferred and heart-sickness lead to unbelief and cynicism- usually disguised as "wisdom and humility". Usually this does not happen overnight. Solomon wrote:

Hope deferred makes the heart sick, but a longing fulfilled is a tree of life (Proverbs 13:12).

As people age over the years, bitterness and hope deferred tend to grow with one small disappointment after another- often beneath our ability to perceive it. A decade later, a vibrant fiery heart willing to risk it all to love Jesus is now lukewarm, calculating and calloused- but at least their Christianity still looks respectable in the eyes of men.

Meanwhile, the older "wiser" believers (often influenced by the sting of the Prince of Greece) then see a young believer stepping out in truly Biblical but apparently "risky" faith. We immediately interpret their actions as being "arrogant" (through our distorted viewpoint of hope deferred, disappointment, and unbelief). Then when God is using them to do great and marvelous things under the anointing of His Spirit, we then judge and slander them to the rest of the Body of Christ under the guise of "caution" and "discernment", causing great wounding to their hearts. A generation gap ensues where holy wisdom is separated from holy passion.

When they inevitably fail because of a lack of humility or wisdom, we are there to give them the "I told you so." A disappointed, broken-hearted, and wounded generation then passes their experiences down to a generation following them. A culture of "safe faith" is nurtured within the Body of Christ. Faith outside the theological boxes is discouraged and even denounced as dangerous. Eventually this culture of "safe faith" turns into practical humanism as the supernatural fire is gone.

While not attempting to give all the answers, we need to look at the fickle crowds of Israel for answers from Palm Sunday to Passover to begin to address this issue of bitter pain of heart-sickness.

Fickle crowds: "Hosanna in the Highest" to "Crucify Him!"

How could the crowds go from exuberant praise to wanting to torture the same man to death in only four days? A simple answer would be unseen angels and demons; Angels energized the crowds to praise him on "Palm Sunday". Demons then energized the crowds to curse and reject him on Passover. Angels and demons were clearly involved but they do not tell the whole story behind the sudden turn-around.

When Jesus rode into Jerusalem on a donkey, the atmosphere was filled with Messianic fever. The Jewish people had been raised with generation after generation suffering under oppressive Gentile nations- first it was Babylon, then Persia, then Greece, and now Rome was even worse. In the midst of the general oppression over generations, at least one leader from all of these kingdoms tried to completely wipe out the Jewish people.

The corporate consciousness of the people was also dominated by prophetic promises of generations past. They would inherit the land. They would be the head of the nations and not the tail. There would be abundant prosperity, freedom, and safety in the land. They were God's special, chosen people above other nations of the earth. Out of the overflow of their blessings, they would be able to lead the nations (by blessing them), and be held in great honor by all of the people groups of the world.

The prophetic promises and decrees for Israel had been dramatically confirmed with the most dramatic events imaginable- crossing the Red Sea on dry land, the audible voice of God from the mountain, manna from heaven, the collapse of Jericho's walls and so many other stories of miraculous deliverance and power.

God had been promising a warrior King like David for centuries. Like David, this warrior Messiah would lead the Jewish people to victory and to eternal prosperity. David and Solomon's rule was the high point in their national history. The people enjoyed prosperity, freedom, and peace. No one dared attack them. Other heads of state visited them including the Queen of Sheba. The glory of God was openly revealed in the temple as the people rejoiced greatly.

Since that time, people were looking for the glory of Solomon's kingdom led by a man like David. The common people had quite possibly heard about Daniel's prophecy of "70 weeks" (Daniel 9:27) related to the Messiah and the Kingdom of God. Generations had been counting the years and the 70 weeks of years were almost up. Surely the Davidic Kingship and Messianic promises were about to come to pass!

In this historical context, the reports began to trickle in: There was the supernatural star in the sky along with reports of shepherds being frightened by an angelic choir. Then a fiery preacher named John emerged from the wilderness crying out, *"Prepare the way of the LORD."* His birth story related to Zechariah's encounter in the temple with Gabriel was stirring up controversy and hope as well.

With Messianic fever extremely high, the reports about Jesus were beginning to flood in among the common people: Lepers were being cleansed, blind eyes opened, and demons were running in horror. Five thousand people had been fed supernaturally- bringing back memories of the manna from heaven. People loved his teaching as he taught as one with authority. People were getting cut to the heart but embracing his Kingdom of God message. To top things off, Lazarus had just been raised to life after being dead for 3 days. Hosanna in the highest! Surely, the promised deliverance of Jerusalem from the Romans is coming. Prosperity at last!

As the crowd gathered and saw Jesus shattered and broken from the Roman whips, everything they had hoped for in Him was shattered as well. No apparent end to Roman oppression coming. No apparent end to the grinding poverty coming. No prominence of the Jewish kingdom now. Perhaps more than one pilgrim witnessing the disillusioning sight said, *"The Messiah should be judging the Romans and they should be in chains- if Jesus is the Messiah, why is He standing before us in chains?"*

Broken-hearted and disillusioned, the religious leaders and elders gave the people a plausible explanation: *"Jesus is a supernatural deceiver who finally reaped what He sowed when Judas betrayed him. He's no Messiah!"* The Bible simply says,

"But the chief priests and elders persuaded the crowd to ask for Barabbas and to have Jesus executed" (Matthew 27:20).

Deeply disillusioned, disappointed, and embittered the crowd shouted, **"Crucify Him!"**

Out of this lasting deep disappointment and hope deferred, and mistreatment by Gentile Church, the Jewish people are a hardened people group against Jesus. Not even reports of the Jesus' resurrection and continued reports of miraculous signs and wonders done by the apostles could change the deep disappointment and hurt in the hearts of the Jewish people. Paul wrote,

Israel has experienced a partial hardening in part until the full number of Gentiles come in. (Romans 11:25)

Where was God in the middle of this huge disappointment?

The people were ready to receive their full inheritance of the prophetic promises, but God knew that they could not steward them and it would ultimately end badly. As we found in the last chapter, when God exalts individuals or a group of people, human conceit tends to develop quickly and grow exponentially as well.

The prophetic promises had clear stipulations. Deuteronomy 4-8 clearly stated that the full release of the prophetic promises was contingent on the people would follow all the commands (beginning with loving God with their whole heart). Deuteronomy 28:1-14 repeated this point-only by whole-hearted full obedience could they receive the prophetic promises from God and enjoy them forever.

The problem was not the prophetic promises of God, but the overall condition of the human heart to receive these promises. God even foretold of the rebellion of his people in Deuteronomy 32:13-22. Basically the release of the prophetic promises would lead to increasing degrees of sin to the point of forgetting about God-because of the sinful heart of humanity. This self-centered conceit, rooted in the "the wisdom of satan" would lead to destruction.

In Matthew 23, Jesus rebuked the religious leaders for their show of hypocrisy. However, the rebuke was far deeper than just related to the religious leaders. The whole nation had a false illusion of what life would be about under the reign of King Jesus. While the nation felt they were ready for the "Day of the Lord" judgments, from God's perspective the hypocrisy openly being displayed by the actions of the religious leaders was (and is) lurking in the heart of all the people. Even the disciples argued about who would be first.

Without a change at the heart level, the people could not receive the prophetic promises and enjoy them forever. However, God announced through the prophets that he would intervene-

"This is the covenant I will make with the house of Israel after that time," declares the LORD. "I will put my law in their minds and write it on their hearts. I will be their God and they will be my people. No longer will a man teach his neighbor, or a man his brother, saying 'Know the LORD,' because they will all know me, from the least of them to the greatest," declares the LORD. "For I will forgive their wickedness and will remember their sins no more."(Jeremiah 31:33-34)

"They will be my people and I will be their God. I will give them singleness of heart and action, so that they will always fear me for their own good and the good of their children after them. I will make an everlasting covenant with them: I will never stop doing good to them, and I will inspire them to fear me, so that they will never turn away from me. I will rejoice in doing them good and will assuredly plant them in this land with all my heart and soul."(Jeremiah 32:38-41)

For I will take you out of the nations; I will gather you from all the countries and bring you back into your own land. I will sprinkle you with clean water on you and you will be clean; I will cleanse you from all your impurities and from all your idols. I will give you a new heart and put a new spirit in you; I will remove from you your heart of stone and give you a heart of flesh. And I will put my Spirit in you and move you to follow my decrees and be careful to keep my laws. You will live in the land I gave your forefathers; you will be my people and I will be your God. (Ezekiel 36:24-28)

God had a plan to confront the false illusions and break open the only way to receive the prophetic promises before the whole issue would come up. God is able to fulfill His perfect plans without violating anyone's free will. The heart of Judas as a betrayer was known by God and included in the plan. God deliberately hid Judas from his disciples so he could execute the evil of what was on his heart. Even Judas's evil could not stop God's grand redemptive plan to confront their false illusions and break open the only way to receive the prophetic promises in Christ Jesus.

God had carefully calculated the extreme disappointment and hope deferred that would result from shattering their illusions. He incorporated their bitter reaction into the plan that included the most humiliating and painful death of His Son as the atoning sacrifice. *God was taking the conceit, disappointment, and anger of their shattered illusions and used it as part of His plan to break open the only way that the Jewish people (and anyone else) could actually receive the prophetic promises of God and enjoy them forever.*

In my case, Pastor Steve and the leadership team had heard correctly from the LORD. What I did not know at the time, was that God had a much greater long-term plan to bring great glory to Him through my life. God wanted to expand my vision beyond the Twin Cities to impact the nations of the earth. This would also require growth in grace as well. Two years later, I would join the IHOP-KC staff as an intercessory missionary; commissioned by a local church in the Twin Cities.

A generation who overcomes hope deferred

In our day, I believe God will raise up a generation that overcome the deep disappointment and hope deferred. The prophet Zechariah brought a message of hope to the Jewish people struggling under oppression and difficult circumstances. He prophesied of a great battle to come:

Rejoice greatly, O Daughter of Zion! Shout, Daughter of Jerusalem!
See, your king comes to you, righteousness and having salvation,
gentle and riding on a donkey, on a colt, the foal of a donkey.
I will take away the chariots from Ephraim and the war-horses from Jerusalem,
and the battle bow will be broken.
He will proclaim peace to the nations.
His rule will extend from sea to sea and from the River to the ends of the earth.
As for you because of the blood of my covenant with you,
I will free your prisoners from the waterless pit.
Return to your fortress, O prisoners of hope;
even now, I announce that I will restore twice as much to you.

I will bend Judah as I bend my bow and fill it with Ephraim.
I will rouse your sons, O Zion, against your sons, O Greece,
and make you like a warrior's sword. (Zechariah 9:9-13)

God is currently at work in raising up forerunners who overcome this insidious ploy of the enemy related to disappointment and hope deferred.

For example, Daniel and Levi Lim have a tremendous heart for the people in Myanmar. In May 2008 a terrible cyclone struck Myanmar and killed over 125,000 people. The whole infrastructure was devastated in the Myanmar delta region. Myanmar shut down global aide from the west (the United States, England, Germany etc.) for political reasons.

Meanwhile, almost simultaneously, China experienced a devastating earthquake that killed another 50,000 people. China, as Myanmar's main ally was now unable to help either-as they were dealing with their recovery operations and preparing for the Olympics. North Korea was suffering from famine and unable to help. Myanmar was in the midst of a humanitarian crisis with over a million more in danger from famine and disease-without help from outside.

In the midst of this, Daniel and Levi Lim listened to God and God sent them. Levi went to Myanmar since Levi is originally from Burma. In the summer of 2008, Daniel brought Emma and joined Levi in Myanmar. God had instructed Him to take their youngest daughter, baby Emma or "Emmanuel" Lim.

A day of confrontation arrived with the Myanmar government. Spiritual warfare was also increasing. Levi boldly charged in telling the generals what she wanted so she could help her people. Breakthrough came with the government of Myanmar the day God visited the IHOP-KC prayer room in the midst of a 40-day fast. In the end, *I love Myanmar* was the only relief organization allowed into the nation. In the midst of this crisis, the ruling party was fascinated with Emma: *Why would Daniel and Levi bring their ill daughter Emma to serve us when she could get all of the health care they wanted for her in the United States?*

As the whole drama played out in the summer of 2008, God then inspired Daniel, Levi, Allen, and other leaders to lead the whole community into extravagant giving as well. In the midst of a community of intercessory missionaries, over a million dollars came in for relief for Myanmar. Millions more came in from across the Body of Christ to provide immediate relief and begin rebuilding the devastated infrastructure.

Suddenly in October, horrible news came from Myanmar: Emma was in critical condition. IHOP-KC rallied in prayer, but the news came too late: Baby Emma was gone.

With the unthinkable came a flood of questions. God inspires Daniel and Levi to go to Myanmar, take Emma, and bring relief to Myanmar with many others. In response to their all-out obedience, they buried Emma in Myanmar, allowed by the sovereignty of God. Why?

Daniel and Levi had hoped Emma would grow up to be a missionary to Asia, but now these hopes were permanently crushed. In the midst of hope deferred and disappointment, almost everyone would have drawn back. Broken hearted but determined, Daniel and Levi returned with Samuel later that year to finish the work of Myanmar relief.

Five years later, the impact is obvious. In 340 short days, as a missionary to Burma, Emma had done more to build the Kingdom of God than most missionaries do in a lifetime. A whole bunch of things in Myanmar ended up named in honor of "Emmanuel". God wrote His name on the land of Myanmar and the whole nation has been affected- even to the point of political reform. Such is the fruit of a baby girl and a courageous couple who overcame hope deferred and disappointment.

Veiling the hearts of the Jewish people is deep disappointment and bitterness from 2,000 years ago. Perhaps we are that rare generation that, having overcome hope deferred and unbelief in our own lives, will love and provoke the Jewish people to turn to their Messiah to invite Him back.

16

WORSHIP- THE FINAL BATTLE

It was on July 4th, near the end of yet another 40-day fast for the breakthrough of revival in 2007. I was enjoying the 6pm Worship with the Word set led by Matt Gilman. As the team sang scriptures about the beauty of God described in Revelation 4 suddenly Matt Gilman broke into a chorus:

Holy, Holy…Lord God Almighty! (Revelation 4:8)

At that moment, the magnificent presence of God flooded the whole room and people rose to their feet, hands upraised. At that moment a new song was being birthed. The song *"Holy"* was released in that set. God would send the song around the world.

Before the return of Jesus to the earth, God has promised to release new songs from heaven. The prophet Isaiah saw what God was doing and said,

Sing to the LORD a new song, his praise from the ends of the earth, you who go down to the sea, and all that is in it, you islands, and all who live in them. Let the desert and its towns raise their voices; let the settlements where Kedar lives rejoice. Let the people of Sela sing for joy; let them shout from the mountaintops. Let them give glory to the LORD and proclaim his praise to the islands. (Isaiah 42:10-12)

There are songs of heaven that have not been sung on the earth yet. This is the hour that God is raising up prophetic singers who deeply know and obey Jesus.

Jesus promised that the gospel would go to every tongue, tribe and people group before the end comes (Matthew 24:14). We will have proof that the task of world evangelism has been completed. In Revelation 5 we find a new song from the angels around the throne:

And they sang a new song: "You are worthy to take the scroll and to open its seals, because you were slain, and with your blood you purchased men for God from every tribe and language and people and nation. You have made them to be a kingdom of priests to serve our God, and they will reign on the earth." (Revelation 5:9-10)

This new song around the throne is the signal to let the final battle begin. Jesus has taken the scroll and its time to open its seals.

Worship wars: The final battle at the end of the age

The Book of Revelation ends in a collision of two worship movements. In Revelation 13, satan has his global worship movement:

Men worshiped the dragon because he had given authority to the beast, and they also worshiped the beast and asked, "Who is like the beast? Who can make war against him?" (Revelation 13:4)

This worship movement has all sorts of counterfeit miracles and "pathetic" experiences to confirm it to those who refuse to believe the truth. This worship movement requires everyone to take a mark on their right hand and forehead. This false worship movement gives boldness among its followers to kill anyone who doesn't worship the beast.

Meanwhile, the book of Revelation describes a true worship movement unto the Lamb who was slain and now lives forever. It looks from the natural eye that they are going to lose the worship war against the devil:

He was given power to make war against the saints and to conquer them. And he was given authority over every tribe, people, language and nation. (Revelation 13:7)

The beast seems to have all he resources, most of the people of the earth, the military might, and everything else going for it.

Yet, a remnant of people consumed with the worthiness of Jesus Christ will worship before God. Worship and prayer will not stop day or night. The prophet Daniel saw this:

In my vision at night, I looked, and there before me was one like a son of man, coming with the clouds of heaven. He approached the Ancient of Days and was led into his presence. He was given authority, glory and sovereign power; all peoples, nations and men of every language worshiped him. His dominion is an everlasting dominion that will not pass away, and his kingdom is one that will never be destroyed. (Daniel 7:13-14)

In the midst of the chaos of those final 42 months, they do not stop singing. Lacking resources, the saints are still shouting for joy over God our Savior. In the midst of mistreatment and injustice at its height they do not stop dancing with Jesus upon injustice. Even in the midst of death, the blood of the saints cries out for the life of God to break out and the wisdom of God to be vindicated over the wisdom of satan. Why?

<u>The greatest commandment, the greatest promise:</u>
Throughout human history, people have sought out to experience the highest, the greatest, and the best. In answering the religious leaders, Jesus gave us understanding of what was most important:

"The most important one," answered Jesus, "is this: 'Hear O Israel, the Lord our God, the Lord is one. Love the Lord your God with all your heart and with all your soul and with all your mind and with all your strength.' The second is this: 'Love your neighbor as yourself.' There is no commandment greater than these." (Mark 12:29-31)

In one sense, it is the greatest commandment simply because of the One who said it is the greatest commandment. God can ask this of us because this is how God loves us!
The greatest commandment is also the greatest promise. In our human strength, loving God like this is completely impossible because of the law of sin and death working in our bodies discussed in chapter 6. God promised that he would do something by the power of His Spirit:

Place me like a seal over your heart, like a seal on your arm; for love is as strong as death, its jealousy unyielding as the grave. It burns like blazing fire, like a mighty flame. Many waters cannot quench love; rivers cannot wash it away. If one were to give all the wealth of his house for love, it would be utterly scorned. (Song of Songs 8:5-7)

What is impossible to man will happen under the anointing of the Spirit. In 1 Chronicles 28-29 As an old man, David at the height of his wealth and resources extravagantly gave towards building the temple as an act of worship to God. His leaders and noblemen followed David's lead.

In Psalm 16 we understand that at God's right hand are pleasures forevermore in heaven. In this case, the joy of heaven overtook the earth leaving David overwhelmed:

But who am I, and who are my people that we should be able to give as generously as this? Everything comes from you, and we have given you only what comes from your hand.
(1 Chronicles 29:14)

God promised a Davidic generation that would walk in extravagant devotion to Jesus with all their heart, soul, mind, and strength. They would then experience the greatness of this eternal joy, peace, and glory in the midst of the darkest and most troubling hour in human history.

The Song of the LORD and the vengeance of God

In Revelation 8:1, the seventh seal is opened by the Lamb and the scripture tells us that there is silence on the earth for half an hour. Why? The prophet Isaiah says:

They raise their voices, they shout for joy; from the west they acclaim the LORD's majesty. Therefore in the east give glory to the LORD; exalt the name of the LORD, the God of Israel, in the islands of the sea. From the ends of the earth we hear singing: "Glory to the Righteous One." (Isaiah 24:14-16)

While there is silence in heaven, the volume of worship from the earth is deafening. All of heaven is silent, gazing upon the spectacle on the earth and at the One they are worshipping.

The earth has been devastated by the first six seal judgments: War, famine, disease, and death are ravaging the earth. The nations are in an uproar over what is happening. The saints are being persecuted and killed for the sake of righteousness. The heavens and the earth are shaking under the weight of sin as creation's groan is fully released.

Paul prophesied that God would make known his manifold wisdom to principalities and powers through the end-time Church (Ephesians 3:10-12). In the midst of all the trouble on the earth are the saints singing to God in worship:

Though the fig tree does not bud and there are no grapes on the vines, though the olive crop fails and the fields produce no food, though there are no sheep in the pen and no cattle in the stalls, yet I will rejoice in the LORD, I will be joyful in God my Savior. The Sovereign LORD is my strength, he makes my feet like feet of a deer, he enables me to go to the heights. (Habakkuk 3:17-19).

Loving obedience is complete at every level within the Body of Christ and the supremacy of God's wisdom over the wisdom of satan is in plain view to everyone in heaven and on earth. It is a sign and a wonder before heaven that will be treasured forever.

Events that have been crawling along now proceed in rapid fashion. Speedy justice is released by God against evil from heaven in response to the unstoppable worship on earth:

In that day the LORD will punish the powers in the heavens above and the kings on the earth below. (Isaiah 24:21)

And you will sing as on the night you celebrate a holy festival; your hearts will rejoice as when people go up with flutes to the mountain of the LORD, to the Rock of Israel. The LORD will cause men to hear his majestic voice and will make them see his arm coming down with raging anger and consuming fire, with cloudburst, thunderstorm and hail. The voice of the LORD will shatter Assyria; with his scepter he will strike them down. Every stroke the LORD lays on them with his punishing rod will be to the music of tambourines and harps, as he fights them in battle with the blows of his arm. (Isaiah 30:29-32)

The great war cry of heaven is the great love song from the earth. Even so, Come Lord Jesus!

About the author: Jess Gjerstad

Born in 1976 in Pusan South Korea, Jess Gjerstad was rescued and adopted into the United States. Jess was raised in a Christian family and grew up in the Lutheran Church.

In 1990, Jess had a life-changing encounter with Jesus Christ. This was the first of many supernatural encounters. He also began to sense a call from God to full-time occupational ministry.

In 2003, God called Jess to leave Minnesota and everything familiar to live in Kansas City. Jess joined the staff at the International House of Prayer (IHOP-KC) in 2003 where he continues to the present. In 2004, Jess earned his Masters of Divinity from Bethel Seminary in St. Paul, Minnesota.

Since then, God has sent Jess to several nations on strategic prayer assignments. Jess also travels around the United States, teaching on prayer, evangelism, and spiritual warfare. Jess's hobbies include reading, meteorology, and prayer.

If you are interested for Jess to come and speak at your church or conference, email authorJessGjerstad@gmail.com